MAKING A
ROSE
GARDEN

MAKING A
ROSE
GARDEN

ETHNE CLARKE

GROVE WEIDENFELD

NEW YORK

Published by Grove Weidenfeld
A division of Grove Press, Inc.
841 Broadway
New York, NY 10003·4793

First published in Great Britain in 1991 by
George Weidenfeld & Nicolson Limited, London

Library of Congress-Cataloging-in-Publication Data
Clarke, Ethne.
    Making a rose garden/Ethne Clarke.
    p.   cm.
ISBN 0-8021-1441-5: $22.50
    1. Rose gardens.   2. Rose culture.   3. Roses.   I. Title
    SB411.C56   1992
    635.9'33372—dc20   91–16902
                            CIP

Illustrators Glenda Biggs pp. 38/9, 41, 42/3, 45, 46/7, 49, 50/1,
53, 54/5, 57, 58/9, 61. Lucy Allen pp. 64, 65, 66, 67, 68, 69
Designer Rita Wüthrich

Typeset by Keyspools Ltd
Colour separations by Newsele Litho Spa
Printed in Italy
Bound in Italy

First American Edition 1992

10 9 8 7 6 5 4 3 2 1

Endpapers Bi-colour roses shine through a curtain of fennel.
Half-title There are roses for every garden setting.
Frontispiece The climbing rose 'Leverkusen' garlands the
gateway to the rose garden at Lime Kiln Rosarium, Suffolk.

Opposite The rose garden at The Coach House, Little Haseley.

Pages 80/1 R. *virginiana*

Page 81 inset R. *sericea pteracantha*

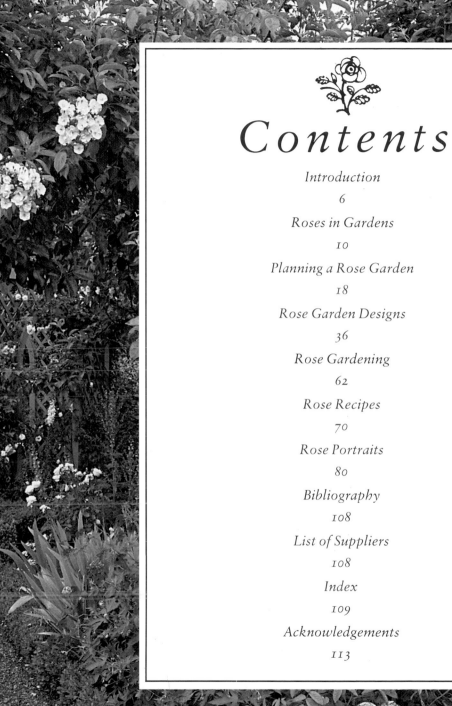

Contents

Introduction

Above The roadside boundary of an apple orchard is given an informal hedge, using bushes of the Gallica rose 'Président de Sèze', and the English Rose 'Constance Spry'.

Previous page Within a frame of tall yew hedges and low box borders, roses serve as the supporting structure of the planting scheme. Rambling roses clothe and soften the hard edges of garden structures, like the arbour *inset*.

When I am asked how I first became interested in gardens, the reply invariably includes a description of my Aunt Helen's garden, and in particular, her rose garden.

Helen lived in a large Georgian rectory in the Malvern Hills and I first came to visit as a child of ten, from the expansive plains of the American Midwest to the soft rolling countryside of western England. Her garden was a relic of the Edwardian golden afternoon, with a vast walled kitchen garden, a croquet lawn framed by herbaceous borders and a formal rosary. My greatest pleasure was to be handed the flower basket and snippers and to go with Aunt Helen into the garden to 'gather a few blooms'. We came back with great bunches of the sweetest scented roses which had flowers, the size of my fist, in every shade from inky burgundy to faint blush pink – and I came

back with the dream that one day I would gather such bouquets from my own English garden.

Now I live in East Anglia and am making the garden I had only before imagined. There are yew hedges, box borders, a kitchen garden with herb edgings, an orchard of 'antique' apple varieties, and roses. At the last count there were 126 bushes, and not many were duplicates. They are mostly old-fashioned shrub roses, species roses and Hybrid Perpetuals, because these are the ones that embody my memories of my aunt's garden. They have the rich perfume, the satin petals in brocade colours, and the graceful demeanour of those languorous times past. I do have an experimental bed of Hybrid Teas and Floribundas, inspired by a bouquet from a friend's Kentish garden. The extrovert colours of the statuesque but perfectly formed flowers look superb in a vase. However, the plants are too stiff to mix well in the borders and so require their own domain, with the result that a corner of the garden throbs like a hammer-struck thumb.

On the other hand, the old roses are perfect border partners. Their muted colours blend well with herbaceous flower colour, and their various habits of growth mean they can be slotted into the garden picture to provide accents, cover gaps, cloak the ground and so on. Old-fashioned roses are more than just a pretty face.

Another major characteristic in their favour is their robust nature. Whereas Hybrid Teas need coddling, the old roses can pretty well resist the most adverse weather conditions, making them ideal for gardeners in cold climates. Also, unlike the Hybrid Teas which must be diligently pruned each season, old roses require an occasional judicious pruning to keep them in trim and in check, as I know to my cost. 'Félicité Perpétue', planted three years ago, has clambered over the stable roof and is starting to push up the tiles. It will have to be brought under control, but not until I see the clusters of tiny, sugar-almond pink flowers littering the dusky-red tiles. Such is the price of glory.

Since this book is as much about making roses part of the garden as making a garden of roses, and the best choice for such a project is the old-fashioned sort, I have focussed on species, shrub, Hybrid Perpetuals and the English Roses created by the rosarian David Austin. The latter are new hybrids of old-fashioned roses and as such retain all the desirable attributes of their parents, but unlike them will flower continually or at least intermittently all summer. Nothing is ever perfect, and if old-fashioned roses have a drawback, it is that some of them flower only once during the summer. But all their other sterling qualities compensate for this shortcoming – if it is one; after all, we do not expect other flowering shrubs to bloom continuously.

Above 'Félicité Perpétue' is a strong-growing rambler that will soon scramble up and over a roof. Roses such as this are useful for camouflage, and can disguise dead trees and any other eyesores with a cloud of luxuriant flowers.

Left Old roses work well in flower borders. Their muted colour and loose habit of growth complement mixed plantings of lavender, campanula, purple sage and various grey-leaved shrubs.

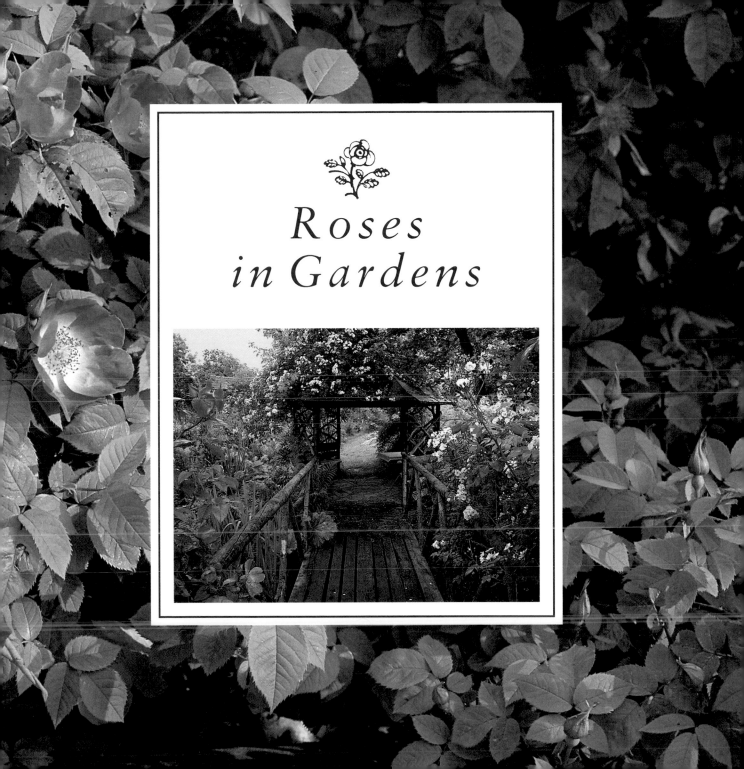

Roses
in Gardens

Previous page Some old roses, like 'Complicata', are hybrids whose origins are lost in the mists of time. The cluster-flowered climber 'Rambling Rector', *inset*, mantling a rustic-work arbour, is another orphan, and has been sheltering in our gardens since *c*.1912. Old-fashioned roses breathe the air of history, and bring romance into our gardens by linking us with the gardens of the past.

Right At Shugborough Hall, seat of the Earls of Lichfield, a rose garden was made twenty-five years ago but in a Victorian style. Characterized by a symmetrical arrangement of geometrically shaped beds, the pattern is given height and emphasis with roses trained as standards and pillars rising out of companion plantings of shrub roses.

It would not be too extravagant to claim that as long as there have been gardens, roses have been cultivated as the most cherished flower. Five millenia ago, Sargon, King of Sumeria, included rose bushes amongst his spoils of war. Roses were praised by the poets of ancient Greece for their grace and perfume, and the Romans used roses with perfumed abandon, stuffing mattresses with pounds of fragrant petals, scattering them over food and drink and bathing in rose-scented water. Early Christians, on the other hand, forbade the use of roses because of their pagan associations. Yet, in time, roses came to be grown in monastery gardens, since the monks used the flowers and hips for medicines, and as a measure of its value made the rose one of the floral emblems of the mother of Christ; the red rose symbolizing her sorrow and the white rose her purity. The Elizabethans gave roses pride of place in the knot garden and in their herbals; 'the Rose doth deserve the chiefest and the most principall place among all floures whatsoever', wrote John Gerard in his *Grete Herball* of 1597. Not surprisingly, when the first gardens were made in the New World, roses were trained along the split rail fences and around the cabin doors. Cabbage roses, York and Lancaster, Apothecary's Rose and wonderfully fragrant Damasks travelled in the Pilgrims' precious cargoes.

In the early 1800s Mr Lewis Kennedy, a London nurseryman, was provided with a special passport that would allow him to travel between England and France to supervise the making of a new garden outside Paris. The two countries were at war at the time, but the garden was Malmaison and it belonged to the Empress Josephine. All hostilities were suspended when it came to supplying her with thousands of species of plants for this great garden. She was determined to have all the then known varieties of rose, some 250 different cultivars, and to make this collection the focus of Malmaison. Today little remains of her fabulous horticultural collection, but there is still a rose garden, and it was Josephine's passion for roses that started the trend for planting gardens devoted entirely to collections of the 'Queen of flowers'.

There are hundreds of different 'species' or wild roses growing all over the world in every kind of habitat, and it was from these roses that the hundreds of old shrub roses have been bred, or simply evolved. There has been much argument over the years as experts try to decide which rose groups to include in the old-fashioned category. For convenience sake, the American Rose Society has advised that 1867, the year the earliest Hybrid Tea 'La France' appeared, be regarded as the dividing line between old roses and modern roses. Beginning with the three oldest types in cultivation, the chief group are:

Alba Roses As early as 1307, the Italian writer Crescentius advised planting a hedge of Alba roses. Over 300 years later, John Parkinson named it the 'most ancient and knowne Rose . . . King of all others'. Its varieties 'Maxima', or Double White, and 'Maiden's Blush' have changed little over the centuries. Albas are always white or faintly tinted pink and the foliage has a pleasing bluish tinge. US zone hardiness: 4.

Damask Roses There are two sorts: the Summer Damasks which flower once in summer and the Autumn Damasks that flower a second time in the autumn. To the former belongs the ancient flower emblem, the York and Lancaster rose, as named by Shakespeare in *Henry VI*. Autumn Damasks are valued for their free-flowering nature and strong fragrance; Herodotus describes these roses as

Once the foremost horticultural collection in the world, Malmaison was created by the Empress Josephine. Her love of flowers, and especially roses, was instrumental in establishing the rose as the foremost garden plant. Today, the garden on the outskirts of Paris retains little of its former grandeur although there is yet a collection of roses, a token reminder of an empress's passion.

growing in King Midas's gardens in Macedonia, and they are included in the fresco decorations of Pompeii. 'Kazanlik' is the Damask raised in Bulgaria to make attar of roses. Damasks have loose clusters of red, pink or white flowers, are richly fragrant, but slightly less hardy than Albas. Zone 5.

Gallica Roses This ancient rose is also named The Rose of Provins after the town in France where it was grown in huge numbers for more than six centuries. It was the basis of an industry which turned the powdered dried petals into conserves, sachets, pastilles and other rose confections, for which it was also known as the Apothecary's Rose. Tradition says that the striped Gallica, Rosa Mundi, is named after the mistress of Henry II, the Fair Rosamond, who had to be hidden at the centre of a labyrinth to protect her from Henry's jealous Queen. Gallicas are perfectly hardy and range in colour from pink to deepest burgundy purple. They flower only once a season, but are worth it for the perfume.

Centifolia Roses Also known as cabbage roses, these are so-called for the masses of petals each flower carries. Cabbage roses are the ones we see in the luscious Dutch flower pieces painted during the seventeenth and eighteenth centuries, although the flowers first appeared in gardens sometime in the late sixteenth century and were probably a cross between an Alba and an Autumn Damask. The very double flower heads weigh down the fine branches so that the bushes have a rather lax habit; their appearance can be improved by growing them over tripod supports or some other framework. Zone 5.

Right The terraces of Powis Castle, Wales, probably date from the late 1600s and are relics of the formal design so popular before the advent of the Landscape movement and 'Capability' Brown. They also face southeast and are sharply drained, so providing an excellent garden site for normally tender plants. The walls are clad in 'Gloire de Dijon' and *R. banksiae* 'Lutea' among others, their honey colour perfectly complementing the warm red of the brickwork.

Moss Roses These are characterized by the sticky, scented, moss-like coating on their stems and sepals. Moss roses first appeared in the mid-eighteenth century as a sport from a Centifolia rose; this is known as *Rosa × centifolia* 'Muscosa' or Common Moss. Other Moss roses are sports from Damask roses. The two can be distinguished by the colour of the moss; Centifolia moss is bright green and abundant on calyx and stems, while Damask moss is sparse and brownish. Some Moss roses grown on their own roots will sucker freely and so should be placed with care in the garden. All sorts are wonderfully scented, with flowers ranging in colour from white to deepest maroon. The Damask Moss is repeat-flowering.

Portland Roses Named for the 2nd Duchess of Portland, these roses are the result of a cross between an Autumn Damask and the Apothecary's Rose, *Rosa gallica officinalis*, carried out in an effort to develop a repeat-flowering rose. The flowers are richly scented, fully double and range in colour from pink through to dark crimson. The bushes are neat and low growing. Zone 5.

China Roses These roses first appeared in European gardens in 1792, brought from the Orient where they had been cultivated for centuries. The first to grace our gardens was 'Slater's Crimson China' followed a year later by Parsons' Pink China, now named Old Blush. Chinas bloom almost continuously which ensured their warm welcome from European horticulturists. The flowers tend to be faintly scented, single or loosely double on small bushes. Chinas are not particularly hardy. Zone 7.

R. 'Alba Maxima' is one of the oldest roses in gardens. Grown in Roman gardens, it was described by a thirteenth-century scholar, appears in paintings by Italian cinquecento masters and in Dutch flower pieces of the eighteenth century and was recognized by sixteenth-century herbalist, John Parkinson, as the 'most ancient and knowne Rose ... King of all others.'

Tea Roses These originated with a hybrid in ancient China that arrived in Europe in the early 1800s. Further hybridization with the Hybrid Perpetuals eventually gave rise to the Hybrid Tea rose. Tea roses, like their near relatives the China roses, are not reliably hardy, to zone 7, but have larger flowers in shades of pink, apricot, and buff to pale yellow, borne continously on small bushes.

Bourbon Roses They were first recorded as growing on the Ile de Bourbon (now Réunion) off the east coast of Madagascar in the trading lanes between Europe and the Orient, a chance cross between the China rose, *Rosa* × *odorata* and an Autumn Damask, which were roses grown as mixed hedges by the island's

inhabitants. The first Bourbon rose was raised from seeds sent to Paris, and was later painted by Redouté in 1824. From its parents the Bourbon inherited fine scent, good shape, a clear pink colour and dependable repeat-flowering; characteristics it has passed on to its many descendants. Zone 5.

Hybrid Perpetuals *The* garden rose from about 1840 to 1880, and the forerunner of the Hybrid Tea rose. The HT roses grabbed the limelight, but the HP roses have continued to be grown for their delicious perfume, wonderful colouring and the beauty of their flower shapes. Hybrid Perpetuals respond well to pegging as they tend to throw up long coarse shoots, and training them laterally will encourage masses of flowers to break all along the stem. Zone 4–5, with protection in the coldest regions.

Noisette Roses The first Noisette was raised in 1802 in South Carolina and named 'Champneys' Pink Cluster'. This was a climber with, as the name suggests, pink flowers borne in clusters. It flowered only once, but was used by the Charleston nurseryman, Phillipe Noisette, to breed the climbing Noisettes, some with clove-scented flowers in tints of blush, cream, ivory and pale yellow. These are delicate roses, not fully hardy and require a warm wall and shelter to give of their best. Zone 7.

The remaining roses which may be styled 'old-fashioned' include the **Hybrid Musks**, raised in the 1920s by crossing a rose named 'Trier' with various Hybrid Teas. The shrubs are tall, repeat-flowering and hardy in zone 4–5.

Rugosa hybrids are a mixed bunch, some repeat-flowering, some only once-flowering, some making huge colourful hips, others none at all. Although Rugosas are the fall-back rose for very cold gardens and will even grow in sandy soil and resist sea spray, choose carefully, since not all cultivars are reliable.

The species *Rosa eglanteria* (**synonym *R. rubiginosa***), the sweet eglantine rose of Shakespeare, has been hybridized to produce a wide variety of mostly single, once-flowering roses ranging in size from 1.2 to 3.6 m (4 to 12 ft). But their greatest value is their scented foliage. Zone 5.

The English nurseryman, David Austin, introduced the first of his **English Roses** in 1961 with 'Constance Spry'. He styles these as 'new roses in the old tradition' and by crossing modern varieties with old roses has created a new race of roses that combines the recurrent flowering and broad colour range of modern roses with the fragrance and elegance of the antique flowers. They are sturdy plants and hardy to zone 4.

Finally, we must not neglect the **species roses**. Without them we would not have such an abundance of choice, or the opportunity they offer to raise a wide variety of flowering shrubs that will add exciting shapes and textures to the garden picture, as well as colour in the garden all year round.

A sport from the antique Gallica rose 'Tuscany', which has been grown since before 1500, the double-flowered 'Tuscany Superb' was introduced in 1848. Because it is slightly more robust and has more deeply coloured, highly scented blossoms than its parent, 'Tuscany Superb' is more widely grown.

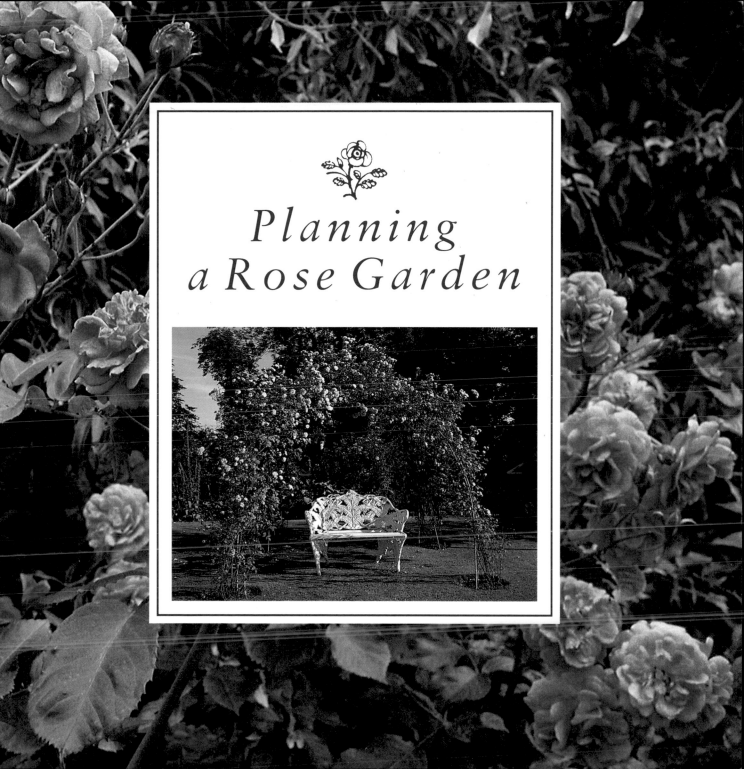

Planning
a Rose Garden

Right Informality and *far right* formality are the two sides of garden design's coin and by spending it thoughtfully in the layout of a garden, a mood can be heightened or a special effect created. The informal use of rambling roses in loudly contrasting colours, showering over ramshackle doors, matches the comfortable feeling of a kitchen garden. By contrast, the formal courtyard of Folly Farm, designed by Edwin Lutyens, is supported by the uniform plantings of soft-pink shrub roses, framed with lavender hedges and bergenia foundation plantings around a central pedestal.

Previous page The rose 'Lavender Lassie' grown against the grey-foliaged Weeping pear, *Pyrus salicifolia* 'Pendula', illustrates colour harmony and also the effectiveness of contrasting leaf shape and texture. *Inset* Sometimes the simplest treatments are the most effective.

There was a time when a rose garden was just that, a separate area of the garden planted entirely with roses set out in formal beds. These were invariably arranged in some sort of repetitious pattern (concentric rings were a great favourite) with little regard to colour or to the quality of accompanying planting, if there was any to speak of. Such plantings can still be seen today in public parks and Gardens of Remembrance – hardly the image we wish to invoke in our own gardens – although the design and planting of rose gardens within private large formal gardens is, fortunately, now generally handled more sensitively.

Roses are flowering deciduous shrubs. While they have an enormous contribution to make to the composition of the garden picture, they can not be relied upon to establish the framework. For that purpose we must use trees and evergreens with roses incorporated into the surrounding plantings of shrubs, herbaceous perennials and annuals.

First Steps

For most of us, our gardens are extensions of our houses; outdoor rooms in which we work (at gardening), rest and play. The decision-making processes involved in designing a garden in which the planting scheme will make the most of a display of roses, are not dissimilar to those employed when deciding how to decorate the interior of a house. You have to consider the scale of the garden, whether or not there should be a period feel to the setting, if there are any special features which could be emphasized, and the sort of atmosphere you wish to create. This is most important, for by manipulating the form, texture and colour of the plants you use, including the roses, it is possible to impart either a feeling of dignified serenity, using the principles of classical formality in which all the elements either side of the centre are mirror images of one another, or the easy informality and gleeful disarray of a cottage garden, where there is a little bit of this and a powdering of that, and each element in the scheme is a separate incident.

Often the direction you take will be decided by the period of the architecture of the house around which the garden is set. Is the building genuinely Tudor or Georgian, a Victorian terrace or modern? Every architectural style has its own inherent design format, and it is within this format that you have to work. This is especially true if you are making the rose garden in a small courtyard or on a terrace where the garden is most intimately related to the house.

Previous page At Hillbarn
House, in the west of
England, an area of the
garden is devoted to a
formal parterre created
from clipped box hedges,
the segments filled with
masses of pink and white
Hybrid Musk roses.

Left The formality of this
garden room, divided
into four equal beds of
roses by crossing paths, is
accented by the edging of
clipped box spheres.
They in turn echo the
detail of the obelisk that
is the focal point of this
area.

Far left Areas of yew-
hedged formal garden are
linked by gravel paths.
Openings in the hedging
frame vistas such as this,
which has been accented
by the climbing rose
'American Pillar' trained
over a wire frame.

Formal Design

The ordered elegance of a formally designed
house demands a balanced, somewhat reser-
ved display in the garden. It is unlikely that a
clutter of beds arranged in random assort-
ment or a scheme planted with the gay
abandon of a wild garden would be a suitable
choice. Such a setting requires vistas and
geometrically designed flower beds in which
the plantings of roses and supporting plants,
while varied in content, are repeated in shape.

This style of garden design is most restful as
the eye is not urged to dart from one focal
point to another. It follows a carefully
ordered path, in which there are few surprises;
all is well-mannered. Within this sort of
structure, background plantings of evergreen
shrubs and trees, which can be trained and
pruned, are always successful. Bay trees
clipped into shapes like pyramids and balls
are particularly effective. Fruit trees can also
be trained and box can be clipped into
geometric topiary; evergreens with columnar
habit, like Irish yew or *Juniperus* 'Skyrocket',
are also popular choices for this sort of
planting. These can be interplanted with roses
chosen for their restrained habit of growth, or
ones which have been trained over a tripod or
trellis frame to make pillars. Ground-covering
roses can be used at the front of plantings, to
soften hard edges and to intermingle with
neatly shaped shrubs like the silver-leaved
Santolina chamaecyparissus.

But no matter how formal the plan of the
garden and the arrangement of the plants
within it, the effect will never be austere, and
while you may have to exercise some restraint
in the variety of plants included, it does not
mean that the garden will appear boring.
Within a formal design there is a great deal
which can be done by contrasting or harmonizing plant textures and colours.

Informal Design

As the term implies, this approach to design is much more casual and ideally suited to a relaxed cottage style of architecture and gardening in which the various elements do not follow such an ordered pattern. This is the setting for vividly coloured herbaceous borders where hollyhocks, irises, lilies, foxgloves and the simple flowers of the cottage garden grow through the branches of a sprawling Bourbon rose like 'Mme Isaac Pereire'. The path to the kitchen could be hedged with a striped Gallica like Rosa Mundi. An informal plan gives scope for amusing visual incidents,

Right 'Paul's Himalayan Musk' engulfs an ancient fruit tree, replacing its harvest with a crowd of scented blossoms assembled in wild profusion; an informal planting that would be difficult to better. The Gallica rose, 'Complicata', fills the foreground.

Far right At Kiftsgate Court, Gloucestershire, twin hedges of Rosa Mundi and *Rosa gallica* control the lavish array of shrub roses within their borders and impose a formal layout on informal plantings.

26

Far right Across the road from Kiftsgate is Hidcote Manor. Begun in 1905, its gardens were instrumental in popularizing the neo-Renaissance style of garden design, that married the formal layouts of quattrocento Florentine villa gardens with informal mixed planting, as typified by the rose walk.

Below The rose-covered pergola at Little Thakeham, West Sussex, is focused on the house.

like a rambling rose tumbling through the boughs of a tree; in one of my favourite gardens, the bust of a Roman emperor is garlanded each summer by one purposely trained branch of the deep red Hybrid Perpetual 'Empéreur du Maroc'.

However, it is just as well to settle on one unifying 'theme' or ingredient when styling an informal planting, for the garden can be unsettling if there are too many disparate elements shouting for attention. This scheme becomes the key note and can be pitched toward plant colour, texture or form.

Before we look at these three important aspects of designing with plants, there is one more area of overall garden design to consider: shape. The combined outline of the plants used within the framework of the garden plan is most important. For example, if the plot is long and narrow it would be a mistake to use too many plants whose habit is tall and narrow – either naturally or, in the case of roses, trained up a framework – in a plan of long narrow beds. The effect would be like looking down a long corridor, your eyes constantly moving from top to bottom without ever taking in the sides. But by including plants with soft rounded habits or spreading horizontal shapes in a plan that emphasizes the horizontal, the illusion of width is created.

Form, Texture and Colour

At this stage in creating the garden, the fun really begins; we settle down to choose the plants, just as in designing an interior we spread out the pattern books, fabric swatches and paint charts.

But where do you begin? There are so many groups of plants to choose from, so many ways of using them, and so many avenues to explore that it can be quite daunting. Do not despair; it is not as difficult as some garden designers would have us believe. First of all, understand that when planning any type of garden, including a rose garden, you work from the general to the specific. In other words, do not think you must immediately decide exactly which varieties of roses and other plants you will use; what you must have is a general idea of the sort of shapes you require.

Form

All plants from the tiniest dwarf alpines to the most statuesque trees have form. They are tall and narrow, low and spreading, short and dumpy; it is their habit of growth. Seen in combination they comprise the shape of the

The pale mauve shimmer
of young budding
wistaria blossoms
contrasts with the depth
of colour of a Moss rose,
while harmonizing with
its hue.

planting, as described above.

When setting out to compose a rose garden, begin by establishing visually pleasing groups of shapes. Sketch the outline of the garden and how it relates to the house: where is the garden entrance from the house, from which windows can the garden be seen, are there paths which are used more than others, is there a main axis (it helps to have one) and are there any features in the neighbouring landscape you need to screen because they are ugly, or, if attractive, could 'borrow' by framing with your planting scheme? Where do you require vertical or horizontal emphasis, and which areas should be left as voids – spaces where there are no visual stimuli?

On a tracing paper overlay, pencil in the shapes. When you have decided on a scheme, you can then begin transplanting the various shapes into their component plant forms. For example, a planting either side of the end of a walk may require an upright shape with a low-spreading mound at its base to put a nice finishing touch to the end of the vista; translate this into a garden seat, planted at each side with a fastigiate evergreen and a skirt of a ground-covering rose like 'Max Graf'.

Texture

You can now apply texture to the forms. Look at the leaves of a sage bush or lavender and compare them to those of a holly or bay. It is the difference between dull and shiny. Dull surfaces absorb light and shiny ones reflect it, and subjects that absorb light visually recede, while those that reflect advance. So if, for example, you wish to emphasize part of the garden, use reflective textures; conversely, use light-absorbing textures to de-emphasize areas of the design.

Texture also refers to the collective appearance of flower and foliage; broad-leaved plants appear smooth, while small-leaved plants look rough and bitty. Graham Stuart Thomas, in his excellent book *The Old Shrub Roses*, writes: 'The old roses create a delightful pattern of flower and foliage at six yards' distance, but at a greater distance give a rather spotty effect.' Their leaves are small in comparison to those of other shrubs and since their flowers are most typically arrayed down their branches, his advice to provide a contrast of other leaf and flower shape is most important. Spikes of white foxgloves, spiky silver sea holly, tall-growing Madonna lilies, the strappy leaves of iris and sisyrinchium, grey-foliaged plants like sage, and broad-leaved hostas and bergenias are all his recommendations for this kind of counterpoint texture.

Colour

Finally, it is time to think about colour. Most of us are aware of the visual tricks which can be played by the clever use of colour harmonies and discords. Some of these pranks have a place in the garden scheme.

The most obvious is the use to which cool colours (blues and greens) and warm colours (reds, yellows and oranges) can be put. The basic rule is that cool colours recede, warm colours advance. Looking again at a long narrow garden, by concentrating the reds, yellows and oranges at the far end, you can make it appear closer. Similarly, blues, purples and greens will make it seem more distant.

Colour creates atmosphere. Warm colours can be used to bring warmth to a north-facing garden, while silvers and blues introduce the coolness of a mountain spring to a sun-baked courtyard. If your courtyard garden seems like the Black Hole of Calcutta, use cheerful yellow roses and plants with golden variegated foliage to suggest sunshine. You can even use colour to accent a theme; for example, if you wish to give your garden a sunny Mediterranean appearance, think of the flower colours you encounter in those regions. They are vivid and flaming, competing with the sun for attention. How unlike the English garden where the tints are muted in shades of delicate pink, mauve and blue.

When selecting the colour for climbing roses it is also necessary to consider the surroundings. The colour of the building is important; co-ordinating the flower colour to that of the brickwork or any other building material is just as necessary as matching furnishing fabric to wall paint. Red flowers against red brick, for example, is a combination fraught with difficulty, as was pointed out by Vita Sackville-West who accused certain flowers of 'screaming' at the brickwork.

Yet colour in the garden is the most transient element of the design, because we normally associate garden colour with flowers. But flowers fade and so they really should not be relied upon as the sole source of vitality in a scheme. Fortunately, there are many plants with coloured foliage which provide interest when the spotlight of the season shifts. Visit your nearest botanical garden and take a good look at the enormous colour variations there are in leaf and, to a lesser degree, in stem. Use these plants as the backbone to a design scheme, calling upon the flowers to augment the display.

Planting Schemes

There is just one other influence that might affect the way in which you decide to make a garden of roses: you may wish to create the garden around a theme. The garden designs in the next chapter are given titles, but they relate more to the types of roses recommended under each heading: the Heritage Garden includes the oldest of the shrub roses, the ones grown in the earliest English and American gardens; the Victorian Rose Garden is full of China roses and Hybrid Perpetuals; the Cottage Garden has climbers and ramblers; in the Scented Garden are the most fragrant roses, including modern English Roses and those for making pot pourri; the Garden for All Seasons has long-blooming roses and species roses that produce colourful hips and foliage in autumn; and the Terrace Garden describes small roses that will not object to being grown in a container, and that can be used to make

The clematis 'Niobe' repeats the shade of pink deep within the newly opened flowers of the climbing rose 'Zéphirine Drouhin'.

low-growing masses. Using the information in these sections, it should be easy to develop your own theme, or enlarge on the suggestions made.

For example, you may work away from home all day, so a courtyard garden that includes a selection of plants which give off their scent in the early evening would provide a grateful welcome home. Also, evening light, which in northern countries tends to be violet, gives a silvery luminosity to pastel and white flowers. This is fortunate since many of the finest scented plants have pale-coloured flowers which harmonize well with the deep red, most fragrant roses.

As well as roses grown around the entrance, tubs clustered about the door, containing sweetly fragrant Mexican orange, *Choisya ternata*, with glossy evergreen leaves and white blossoms; *Daphne × burkwoodii* 'Somerset', or *D. odora* 'Aureomarginata', with golden variegated leaves and terminal clusters of delicious pink flowers, are especially good. Many of the lilies are most strongly fragrant in the evening and as Mr Thomas points out, are good companions to old roses. Among the annuals, look for dwarf strains of nicotiana, particularly white- and green-flowered strains for these are the most strongly scented, and do not forget night-scented stocks.

Adhering to a theme for a garden of roses would require some pleasant hours spent browsing in garden design and history books, looking for information as well as for inspiration, but it would certainly help you to think of many original ways in which to use the many different sorts of roses at your disposal.

Far left At Elsing Hall, Norfolk, the terrace is bathed in afternoon sun, its warmth and bright aspect enhanced by plantings of the shell-pink rose 'Fantin-Latour', and button-sized flowers of golden-leaved feverfew. When treated as a climber it is even more inclined to produce clusters of the sweetly scented blooms.

Left The steely-blue foliage of rue and purple-leaved sage provide the perfect contrast to the fiery orange tints and ruby-red hips of 'Corylus'.

Following page Border plantings of the Moss rose 'William Lobb' with *Rosa californica* 'Plena' at Park Farm, Great Waltham, Essex. While the flowers' colours are similar, their sizes and the texture and style of the foliage offer an effective contrast. The *inset* shows roses growing in the streamside wild garden at Lower Brook Cottage, Suffolk.

Rose Garden Designs

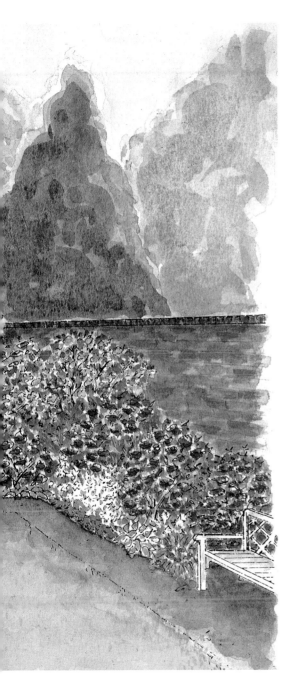

Heritage Garden

Early nineteenth-century American gardens were, like their British relations, a satisfying partnership of formal and informal elements. Formal lawns and borders were nearest the house, and small groves of ornamental trees lay beyond with shaded gravel walks snaking around the lawns below the leafy canopy. In gardens such as these, the oldest of the old roses are most at home.

In this garden the parterre consists of two squares of grass bordered by gravel paths. The borders forming the boundaries are backed by brick walls and bisected by the stairs leading down from the terrace, two flights of stairs opposite leading up to the grove and benches positioned in the centre of the side borders. Each section of border is devoted to one group of roses.

Old striped Gallicas like Rosa Mundi can be used to make cushion hedges either side of the benches. To keep them neat they must be given quite a severe clipping each spring, which encourages masses of new healthy growth and thus defeats mildew attack. Other sections of the side borders are planted with groups of various Gallicas like the dark velvety 'Cardinal de Richelieu' or 'Assemblage des Beautés'.

The space between the steps leading up to the grove is planted with a collection of Damask roses. The tall white-flowered 'Mme Hardy', 'Ispahan' and 'Kazanlik' making the background for bushes of 'Gloire de Guilan' and 'Leda', called the Painted Damask for its double white flowers tipped with deep pink.

The borders either side of the terrace steps are the home of the Alba roses, with stately 'Mme Legras de St Germain' in each corner and masses of pink-flowered 'Königin von Dänemark' below the dogwood trees either side of the steps leading down from the terrace. Between these two groups, the border is planted with bushes of 'Alba Maxima', 'Great

Capped by climbing and trailing roses, mellow stone walls and warm brickwork enhance the repose of formal gardens.

Right Changes in level help to emphasize the different character of the two sections of the garden, as shown here in the rose garden at Arley Hall, Cheshire.

cottage pinks, hollyhocks and Shasta daisies, while foreground planting of viola, hosta and stachys make ground-covering carpets along the path edge. Groups of pink and white tulips are dotted the length of the borders, their fading leaves will be disguised later by the emergent growth of the herbaceous plants and the new growth of the roses.

Below the Damasks the ground is covered with the evergreen periwinkle, *Vinca minor* 'Gertrude Jekyll' and *Alchemilla mollis*. The trailing tendrils of the small shiny leaves of the periwinkle contrast well with the broad, dull grey-green foliage of the alchemilla and, in bloom, the white periwinkle shines like a tiny star amidst the foamy chartreuse flower heads of the alchemilla.

In the grove garden, a central oval lawn is flanked by wings of grass in which are planted a selection of fruit trees. A small fountain pool plays at the head of this garden area. Even though the structure of this space is formal the planting is relaxed and the roses are large billowing masses planted in the corner areas created by the curve of the encircling paths.

In spring the fruit trees burst into blossom and swathes of snowdrops and *Crocus tommasinianus* make islands in the oval lawn, while the 'wings' beneath the fruit trees are home to naturalized narcissi. This area can only be mown after the bulb leaves die back, so it could be sown with a meadow mixture.

Rosa eglanteria (synonym *R. rubiginosa*), the sweetbriar; *R.* × *centifolia* 'Bullata', the 'lettuce-leaved' rose; and *R.* × *damascena bifera*, the repeat-flowering 'Quatre Saisons' are just a few of the roses left to grow in wild abandon above an evergreen carpet of ground-hugging ivy and periwinkle.

Maiden's Blush' and the tall-growing 'Céleste', with its soft pink flowers and wonderfully sweet scent.

Antique roses such as these flower only once a season, so careful thought must be given to accompanying plantings of herbaceous perennials to prolong the summer, bulb plantings to herald the coming of spring and the use of shrubs and trees to provide structure during winter.

In this part of the garden the only trees are the dogwoods, but the roses are underplanted with a thicket of lily-of-the-valley. Their broad shiny leaves are a good contrast to the glaucous foliage of the Albas, and the fragrant white flowers in early summer enhance the soft tints of the roses. White-flowered lilac and philadelphus fill the corners of the garden.

Herbaceous perennials are grown in the side borders among the groups of Gallicas. Tall-growing varieties are planted at the back of the beds, including *Campanula latifolia alba* and *C. persicifolia* 'Snowdrift', aquilegia,

A *Cornus florida* 'Cherokee Chief'
B apple trees in variety
C *Prunus sabhirtella* 'Autumnalis'
D white lilac and/or philadelphus

1 Rosa Mundi
2 'Cardinal de Richelieu'
3 'Assemblage des Beautés'
4 'Ispahan'
5 'Mme Hardy'
6 'Kazanlik'
7 'Leda'
8 'Gloire de Guilan'
9 'Mme Legras de St Germain'
10 'Königin von Dänemark'
11 'Alba Maxima'
12 'Great Maiden's Blush'
13 'Céleste'
14 *R. eglanteria*
15 *R. × centifolia*
16 *R. × damascena bifera*
17 *R. pimpinellifolia* 'Double White'
  a lily-of-the-valley
  b *Vinca minor* 'Miss Jekyll'
  c *Alchemilla mollis*
  d,e,f *Campanula latifolia alba*, *C. persicifolia* 'Snowdrift', aquilegia, Shasta daisies etc.
  g cottage pinks
  h naturalized narcissi

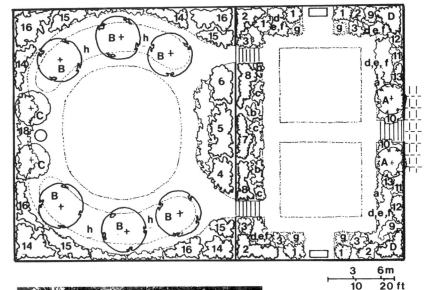

Above Plan for the Heritage Garden based on the gardens of the University of Virginia, which were originally designed by Thomas Jefferson. The modern restorations (by the state's Garden Club) employ many of the plants he would have used, including shrub and species roses.

Behind the fountain, two specimen trees of *Prunus × subhirtella* 'Autumnalis' open their tiny flower pendants at the tail-end of winter to be followed in early summer by the creamy-white flowers of *R. pimpinellifolia* 'Double White', planted around the fountain. This useful low-growing spreading rose has fine ferny foliage and little ebony hips, which provide added interest in autumn.

This garden plan for making use of antique roses provides two distinct areas for their appreciation. The formal area, with its flower borders and massed plantings of rose groups, provides a quiet setting for conversation, which is why the benches are placed here. The grove garden, on the other hand, is for exploring with its secret corners and winding walks.

Cottage Garden

No two words in the gardener's vocabulary are as evocative as 'cottage garden'. Redolent of sweet-scented herbs and simple flowers, they conjure up an image of an unpretentious dwelling wreathed in Tea roses with brimming bowls of pot pourri at the window, made from the rose petals and fragrant herbal foliage. Its garden is as equally unsophisticated, for in its precincts, vegetables and fruit grow cheek by jowl with the choice blossoms of the seed catalogues. More roses ramble along low picket fences and weave through hedgerows. They climb up a sturdy trellis support to garland an arbour over a narrow path or to shade a simple bench. A cottage garden would not deserve its name without an abundance of roses.

Curiously, cottage gardens are conceived as being cultivated with a sort of horticultural mayhem, where beds and borders are filled with wild abandon. In reality, the genuine article is the model of restraint, and a true cottage garden is as tidy and orderly as the home it adorns. One of the most breathtaking gardens I have ever seen was in front of a fifteenth-century, half-timbered thatched cottage in rural Worcestershire in the west of England. Owned by two elderly sisters, it had been their parents' home and the garden had hardly altered in ninety years. The garden area was divided into four rectangular beds either side of a grass walk. Narrow grass paths separated the beds in which the sisters grew onions, cabbages, carrots and countless other vegetables along with clumps of Madonna lilies, 'for the altar, dear', cordons of sweet peas that they sold in bunches from a bucket at the gate, stands of Shasta daisies and dozens of bushes of the most perfumed roses. 'François Juranville' clothed the end wall of the cottage, and the end of each bed where it marked the property line was indicated by a climbing rose on a tripod. Behind the cottage, a rambling rose clambered over the small garden shed. At the

Top Vegetables, herbs and roses in a neatly muddled cottage garden.

Above 'Albertine' trained over the wooden arch and Rosa Mundi in the foreground, frame a cottage entrance.

height of the season the cottage disappeared beneath its floral finery.

The two features that characterize a cottage garden, mixed and informal planting within a symmetrical or otherwise formal frame, can be recognized in 'cottage-style' gardens all over the world, wherever there is a need to combine beauty and utility in a small area.

In this small garden, the idea of symmetrically arranged beds has been translated to a circular pattern of six wedge-shaped beds set within a square and radiating around a central ornament, in this case a bird-bath improvised from a large terracotta saucer on a brick plinth. A beautifully crafted urn or sundial could have been used, but the 'make-do' simplicity of a saucer and a few bricks is more in keeping with the nature of a cottage garden. The paths radiating from the centre are narrow, serving only to divide the beds and provide some access for weeding. They are of gravel laid over heavy-duty black plastic sheeting to prevent grass and weeds

taking root. Pre-cast concrete 'Yorkstone' paving stones or more expensive brick could also be used.

Planting is arranged so that the lowest growing plants are at the centre of the garden, increasing in height to the outer edges. The tallest plants are in the corner beds created by the circle set within the square. Here, the sweet-scented Bourbon 'Blairii No. 2' has been trained up stout oak posts, to be followed in flower by the soft pink blossoms of the clematis 'Comtesse de Bouchaud' supported by the rose branches. This clematis is pruned hard each spring, sending up new flowering tendrils that can be trained over the rose. Using such a clematis ensures that the display never becomes an impenetrable thicket of stems and shoots.

At the end of the side beds, tripods about 1.8 m (6 ft) tall and made of rounded wooden stakes support the climbing Tea 'Gloire de Dijon' and 'Climbing Mme Caroline Testout', a climbing Hybrid Tea. The long stems are coiled around the tripod so that they are trained near to horizontal which encourages flowering shoots to break along their length. The remaining four beds are planted with low-growing bush roses so that the view from the cottage windows along the central path is not obscured. 'Climbing Cécile Brunner' and 'François Juranville' clothe the cottage walls.

Three of the beds are then planted up with a wide variety of simple herbaceous plants and flowering shrubs: *Aconitum* 'Bressingham Spire', *Achillea* 'Moonshine', Shasta daisies, peonies, irises and English lavender at the outer edges; masses of hardy geraniums and grey-leaved artemisia and santolina, rosemary, alchemilla and purple sage in the

A *Choisya ternata*
B *Buxus sempervirens*
C *Osmanthus delavayi*
1 'Blairii No. 2'
2 'Gloire de Dijon'
3 'Climbing Mme Caroline Testout'
4 'Climbing Cécile Brunner'
5 'François Juranville'
6 'Buff Beauty'
7 'Fantin-Latour'
8 'Perdita'
9 'Othello'
a hardy geranium 'Johnson's Blue'
b *Artemisia ludoviciana*
c *Santolina incana*
d rosemary
e *Alchemilla mollis*
f *Salvia officinalis* 'Purpurascens'
g *Aconitum* 'Bressingham Spire'
h *Achillea* 'Moonshine'
i Shasta daisies
j *Paeonia officinalis*
k irises
l English lavender
m thyme
n stachys
o variegated saxifrage
p *Phuopsis stylosa*
q *Alcea rosea*
r *Clematis* 'Comtesse de Bouchaud'
s cut-and-come-again salad
t chives and various herbs
u 'Minibel' tomato
v beetroot, carrots
w spinach, chard etc.

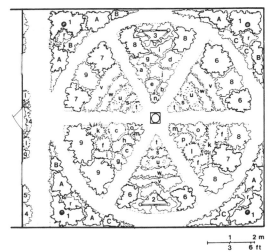

Plan for the Cottage Garden. The square site has been divided into pie-wedge beds, planted with a mix of herbaceous and annual flowers, vegetables, herbs and roses.

Tripods and pillars of climbing and rambling roses give height to the design. An alternative would be to cover the central path with a simple arch pergola.

middle ground; and creeping thyme, stachys, marjoram, variegated saxifrage and clumps of *Phuopsis stylosa* hug the ground at the apex of

each wedge. The other three beds are used to grow a small selection of vegetables, more to add culinary variety than to be self-sufficient. The choice is dictated by interest and size; using cut-and-come-again salad mixtures, chives, miniature 'cocktail' tomatoes, beetroot and carrots, which are sown consecutively and harvested when still small, the gardener makes use of this delightfully decorative yet functional cottage rose garden.

Terrace Garden

The peristyle gardens of ancient Rome were the forerunners of the terrace gardens of our modern cities. The excavation of the ruined city of Pompeii, eerily preserved in volcanic ash that filled every crevice and solidified, revealed the city's elegant houses still intact. Even the very roots of the plants grown in their gardens made moulds in the ash, allowing archaeologists to cast their structure in plaster and to identify them. Pompeian gardens, like modern terrace gardens, were intimate walled enclosures, decorated with water channels and fountains, vine-covered pergolas, clipped box edgings, olive and bay trees and countless roses. Even the surrounding walls were frescoed with rose garlands. But then we have read of the Roman obsession with roses.

Because a terrace is the most immediate garden extension of the house, usually reached through double French windows leading out from the main room, it should be furnished with as much care and discretion as the room it adjoins, and reflect the style of the interior decoration. This is not a trivial consideration; nothing would be more inappropriate than to walk out of a living room, furnished with fine antique furniture, onto a terrace where the seating was moulded white plastic and the plant containers or other ornaments similarly modern.

The temptation with a terrace is to extend the gardening space with a selection of plants growing in a variety of pots, urns and so on. But this, again, requires careful thought as the terrace could turn into a slalom course of shin-abrading terracotta and stone. Keep clutter to a minimum.

It helps if shapes are well-defined; a firm line should be taken with surrounding flower beds, contained perhaps by box edging, rather than allowing plants to trail and droop over the paving to be ground into slippery mush underfoot. But the planting within the edging can be relaxed; mingled groups of herbaceous perennials, annuals and flowering

other plants have retired for the season). Within this frame, the roses, chosen for their habit and colour, are the subject of the garden picture.

Because space is restricted, the roses must have a neat habit and for this reason, some of the English Roses, many of the China roses and some of the smaller growing Bourbons are ideally suited to a terrace garden.

Beneath the standard laurels, low-growing bushes of pink-flowered 'Hermosa' and buff-coloured 'Perle d'Or' are grouped. The pink shadings of the latter enrich the soft tints of the former and together they blend into a fine complement to the dark-flowered, dwarf lavender 'Hidcote' that makes such a spiky purple fringe above the flat-topped box.

'Zéphirine Drouhin' throws her raspberry-

Above The warm shelter of a terrace garden allows you to grow some of the more tender roses, like *Rosa banksiae* 'Lutea'.

shrubs and climbers chosen to complement the roses and prolong the flowering period.

In this city courtyard, the standard double French windows lead onto a terrace paved with buff-coloured slabs. The ornaments include a splash fountain set into a side wall, playing its stream into a shell-shaped basin. On the opposite wall there is a statue. A wrought iron bench in a trellis-made arbour is centred on the wall opposite the French windows. Square wooden 'Versailles' tubs mark each corner.

Plants are used to reinforce the architectural quality of the space; Portugal laurels trained as standards are sited in pairs either side of the fountain and the statue. Any other evergreen would serve the same purpose, providing height to the planting (strong verticals are useful) and year-round interest (it gives substance to the garden when all the

Right A small-stature rose like 'Nozomi' is ideal for container growing; here it is trained as a weeping standard.

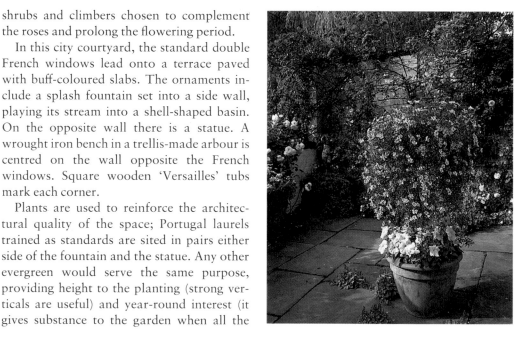

scented blooms over the arbour trellis. This rose is a good choice for a tight space since it is thornless and therefore not a threat to skin or clothing. She is also allowed to extend a few branches against the wall and through these the large-flowered clematis 'Marie Boisselot' threads her way to display her brilliant white blooms in late summer.

If the terrace was particularly warm and sheltered, the temptation to grow a tender rose like 'Maréchal Niel' would be hard to resist. This is the Noisette Tea rose so loved by the Victorians, who went to great lengths to grow it successfully, usually giving it pride of place in the conservatory. Its shapely yellow flowers have a rich perfume; it grows to about 3 m (10 ft) and is repeat-flowering.

The roses in the Versailles tubs are the white-flowered Bourbon, 'Boule de Neige', with a scent, according to Nancy Lindsay, 'as sweet as jasmine on a summer night'. It is almost thornless. A tiny-leaved silver-variegated ivy is clipped neatly about the feet of each rose.

Flowers growing in the adjacent flower beds include purple-flowered foxgloves, *Digitalis purpurea*; variegated hostas; *Liatris spicata*; *Geranium endressii* 'Wargrave Pink'; pink-flowered phlox and white *Aster novae-angliae* 'Herbstschnee'. The tobacco, *Nicotiana langsdorfii* is dotted about as a filler, its tiny lime-green pendant flowers dancing about with each passing breeze. This is a perennial but is usually grown as an annual.

All that remains is to remember that in a small space, neat planning and planting must be kept neat. Dead-head faithfully, guard dutifully against pest and disease and generally run a tight ship.

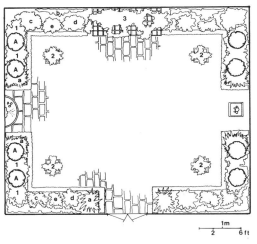

Plan for the Terrace Garden. A feeling of spaciousness is given by keeping the plan simple and uncluttered.

A Portugal laurel standards
1 'Perle d'Or' and 'Hermosa'
2 'Boule de Neige'
3 'Zéphirine Drouhin'
a *Lavandula* 'Hidcote'
b *Clematis* 'Marie Boisselot'
c *Nicotiana langsdorfi*
d *Digitalis purpurea*
e *Geranium endressii* 'Wargrave Pink'

While the plan may be simple, the greatest use should be made of contrasts in plant textures and shapes and the materials used for urns, paving and so on. The pot-grown rose is 'Gertrude Jekyll'.

Victorian Rose Garden

Have not the flowers a language? speak, young rose,
Speak bashful sister of the footless dell!
Thy blooming loves – thy sweet regards disclose

The language of flowers appealed to the romantic sensibilities of the Victorians who revelled in the exoticism of its origins – it was supposedly a dumb language used by ladies of the Turkish harem to convey messages to their illicit lovers – and the *risqué* overtones that could be attached to a simple posy. One little book lists over two dozen types of rose, each with its own significance including: 'Love is dangerous' (Carolina rose), 'Confession of love' (Moss rose bud) and 'Reward of virtue' (crown of roses). Few other floral emblems commanded so many meanings.

Victorian gardeners attached equal importance to roses, devoting great chunks of garden to shaped rose beds. One of the more breathtaking examples, judging from the photographs taken at the time, was the garden laid out in 1872 by W.A. Nesfield for Lady Lothian at Blicking Hall in Norfolk. A 2 acre (1 hectare) terrace on the east lawn and the broad avenue sweeping up to the distant temple were studded with tiny beds cluttered with a myriad of rose bushes, plus roses grown on pillars, chains and tripods. This was in addition to thousands of annuals, perennials, bulbs and whatever else was deemed necessary.

In 1902 Gertrude Jekyll wrote with Edward Mawley *Roses for English Gardens*, setting out quite firmly how she believed roses should be used. At about this time, the vibrantly coloured and tightly corsetted Hybrid Tea roses that we know so well today were making their first appearance; she clearly felt guidance was needed to ensure these roses were used 'appropriately', although her lists included many of the older Hybrid Perpetuals and old shrub roses.

Her ideal rose garden was laid out in a shallow valley, surrounded by an evergreen woodland of yew, holly and Scotch pine, but where the site was a stretch of level ground. Miss Jekyll pronounced, '. . . it will be found a great enhancement to the beauty of the roses and to the whole effect of the garden if it is so planned that dark shrubs and trees bound it on all sides. . .' There should be a central lawn bordered by rose beds, surrounded by broad gravel walks that enter the rose garden at each corner. She recommended that the outer edge of the beds be set with posts and chains supporting pillar and 'cluster' roses placed alternately.

These principles were followed in the plan of this garden enclosure which forms part of a larger scheme. Encircled by a planting of mixed evergreens, including holly, holm oak and Scotch pine, the garden square is outlined by a low yew hedge. The paths are gravel and two-thirds the width of the rose beds. A plain square of lawn is at the centre.

The posts and chains recommended by Miss Jekyll for training climbers and pillar roses are placed in formation at each corner. Following her counsel, each inner and outer corner is planted with a rambler rose so that its branches can clothe the chains either side. The other two posts are furnished with pillar roses. 'The Garland', 'Climbing Cécile Brunner', 'Mme Grégoire Staechelin', 'Félicité Perpétue' and 'Aimée Vibert' are just a few of the ramblers used that might have tempted Gertrude. The beds are devoted to Hybrid Perpetuals and some of the older Hybrid Teas.

'Baron Girod de l'Ain', 'Roger Lambelin' and 'Ferdinand Pichard' have petals tipped and striped with white; 'Baronne Adolphe de Rothschild' (more popularly known as 'Baroness Rothschild'), 'Général Jacqueminot', 'Georg Arends', 'Mrs John Laing' and 'Paul Neyron' are some of the wonderful bushes that fill the beds.

'The gorgeousness of brilliant bloom, fitly arranged, is for other plants and other por-

A mixed plantings of holly, Scotch pine and holm oak
B yew
C lawn
D gravel path
1 'The Garland'
2 'Climbing Cécile Brunner'
3 'Félicité Perpétue'
4 'Aimée Vibert'
5 'Mme Grégoire Staechelin'
6 'Climbing Mme Caroline Testout'
7 'Perle d'Or'
8 'Sombreuil'
9 'Roger Lambelin'
10 'Ferdinand Pichard'
11 'Baron Girod de l'Ain'
12 'Général Jacqueminot'
13 'Baronne Adolphe de Rothschild'
14 'Paul Neyron'
15 'Georg Arends'
a hosta
b Bergenia 'Bressingham White'
c Artemisia 'Powis Castle'
d Salvia blancoana
e Marrubium vulgare
f stachys
g Alchemilla mollis
h hardy fern
i Lavandula spicata
j Dianthus 'Mrs Sinkins'
k Nepeta 'Six Hills Giant'

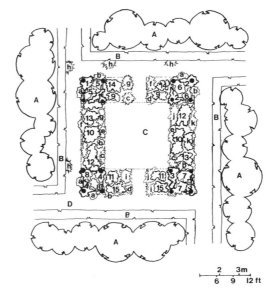

Plan for the Victorian Rose Garden, based on the principles of Gertrude Jekyll. She advised a simple square lawn surrounded by rose beds, screened by dark yew hedges.

tions of the garden; here we do not want the mind disturbed or distracted from the beauty and delightfulness of the Rose.' A difficult edict to obey, and to a degree Miss Jekyll's idea is valid. However, if underplanting is limited to complementary foliage, and other flowering plants banned, the hard edges of the design are softened.

Inevitably, there will be a good north-facing corner where some fern might be tucked at the foot of the hedge. Collections of hosta or bergenia can be lodged within the confines of the post-and-chain corners. *Bergenia* 'Bressingham White' has small oval leaves that colour well in autumn and clusters of clean white flowers in early spring.

Plants of the artemisia 'Powis Castle' make shaggy mounds dotted along the path side of the beds, in company with *Salvia blancoana*, a miniature sage with small, oval, highly scented leaves and *Marrubium vulgare*, or horehound, with soft, round, grey furry leaves.

In a rose garden like this, less is really more, so the temptation to crowd the bushes, or to muddle many different varieties up the corner supports was resisted. Holding to a repeated planting of several varieties gave this garden of roses a sense of unity of purpose.

Scented Garden

If you make a garden including old-fashioned roses, you will in effect be making a scented garden. But if the result you are aiming for is a living pot pourri outside your garden door, then the choice of plants must be dictated by your nose. You must aim to sniff out the flowers and leaves which give freely of their perfume and combine these in an olfactory garden picture, as well as paying attention to the usual visual composition.

For example, the fragrance of the leaves of *Rosa primula*, the Incense Rose, does not travel well, so plant it against a wall near a doorway so that on a warm humid day its perfume can be appreciated at close quarters. This is in contrast to the sweetbriar, *R. eglanteria* (*R. rubiginosa*), and its hybrids like 'Amy Robsart' that wantonly release the ripe apple scents of their foliage into any passing breeze.

For most roses, however, the perfume is in the petals. Nothing can equal the pleasure of burying your nose into a sun-warmed bloom of 'Mme Isaac Pereire'. Its smell of crushed raspberries is characteristic of the Bourbon race. Then you must be able to savour the resiny spice of a Moss rose, to be enjoyed in the scent of the flower and the mossy stems and sepals from which it takes its name; 'William Lobb' is a good start.

'Gloire de Dijon' is an old tea-scented climbing rose of exquisite charm; grow that with a late Dutch honeysuckle as the flowers bear the same tints and the spice of honeysuckle complements the fruity tea perfume of the rose.

This narrow town garden behind a terrace or row house was conceived as a scented enclave. The boundary walls which divide the property from its neighbours help to contain the fragrance of leaf and flower.

The terrace is shaded by a rustic-work pergola covered with *R.*

Right As well as flower scent, some roses have perfumed foliage. *R. primula* has dainty dark green leaves that smell strongly of incense, which gives it the common name, the Incense Rose.

Below Bourbons, Gallicas and Damasks are the roses to grow in a garden devoted to scent.

banksiae 'Lutea'; the south-facing aspect and sheltering walls help this rose to thrive. The clusters of small double flowers have a warm citrusy scent, perfectly complemented by the perfume of the Incense Rose planted against the terrace wall.

From the terrace a narrow path leads down the garden between two opposing garden areas. To one side the narrowest bed is planted with mixed shrubs of santolina, English lavender and catmint, *Nepeta × mussinii* (*Nepeta × faassenii*); plants of white-flowered annual tobacco are dotted throughout the shrub planting so that the evening scented flowers are held high above the grey cushions. Plants of lemon verbena, *Aloysia triphylla*, trained as standards and underplanted with scented leaf geraniums are set out in a row of

tubs spaced evenly down the length of the border. These are tender plants, and in a cold climate must be overwintered indoors. The verbena should be kept dry and in the spring pruned into shape before being returned to its garden position when all danger of frost has past. The geraniums, which include *Pelargonium* 'Royal Oak', *P. capitatum*, *P. tomentosum* and the best scented, 'Mabel Grey', can be brought into the house over winter and kept in a cool sunny place. In spring, trim them up and return them to their outdoor positions.

Opposite, a small square of lawn is bordered by a horseshoe of Bourbon roses underplanted with the hardy geranium *Geranium macrorrhizum*. The leaves have a pungent resinous scent and turn a good colour in autumn, and the flowers in summer are a shade of magenta, not far removed from the

A hornbeam
B lilac
C *Sarococca hookeriana digyna*
D *Philadelphus* 'Lemoinei'
E *Choisya ternata*
1 *R. primula*
2 'Amy Robsart'
3 'William Lobb'
4 *R. banksiae* '*Lutea*'
5 'Mme Isaac Pereire'
6 'Louise Odier'
7 'Reine Victoria'
8 'Mme Pierre Oger'
9 'Gloire de Guilan'
10 'Kazanlik'
11 *R. gallica officinalis*
12 'Zéphirine Drouhin'
a *Santolina incana*
b lavender
c nepeta
d lemon verbena
e scented geraniums
f purple sage
g rosemary
h *Geranium macrorrhizum*
i box

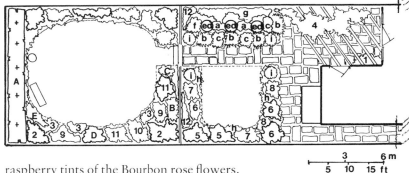

raspberry tints of the Bourbon rose flowers.

Clipped box balls mark the beginning and end of the path where it descends a few steps down to an oval lawn surrounded by a mixed shrubbery that includes bushes of the Damask roses 'Gloire de Guilan' and 'Kazanlik', and *R. gallica officinalis*, the Apothecary's Rose. The Bourbon 'Zéphirine Drouhin' is trained against a trellis that separates this sunken garden from the terrace-level garden. Shrubs grown among the roses include lilac, purple sage, rosemary, winter box, *Sarococca hookeriana digyna*, mock orange, *Philadelphus* 'Lemoinei' and Mexican orange, *Choisya ternata*.

The garden is terminated by a screen of hornbeam, trained with bare trunks to 1.5 m (5 ft) and then clipped to make a solid screen of foliage – a hedge on stilts. The shrub planting gives way to an underplanting mat of variegated ivy that is clipped over periodically to keep it within bounds. The picture is completed with a stone urn positioned on an axis with the end of the path. Next to it a garden bench is placed looking back towards the pergola-covered terrace. On still summer evenings, this bench is a perfect place from which to inhale the breath of the roses and to enjoy the perfection of a garden pot pourri.

Plan for the Scented Garden. From the rose-covered terrace to the seat beneath the stilt hedge, the captured perfumes of leaf and flower can be easily enjoyed.

Left One of the most deliciously fragrant roses is the Bourbon 'Mme Isaac Pereire', with vast double raspberry-pink flowers with a rich fruity scent.

Garden For All Seasons

So much has been written about the importance of having colour and variety in the garden throughout the year, that it hardly needs further description. But it is useful to know that when making a rose garden, you will not be prevented from fulfilling this requirement. There is among the species roses and some hybrids great potential for coloured foliage, cheerful berries and interesting stems; the ornamental triumvirate of the 'winter garden'. Supplement these with a sprinkling of shrubs and trees noted for their out-of-season behaviour and incorporate autumn and early spring flowering bulbs and you have followed the recipe for success.

One of the best winter gardens I have seen is in south-eastern Wisconsin, a north Midwestern state that fully experiences the extremes of climate for which the United States is renowned. It was the dead of winter, snow was blanketing the ground and the garden had been a building site not too many months before. But already there was a firm structure of hedges and evergreens that brought the natural woodland at the far end of the property into the garden picture. A number of the trees and shrubs included had been chosen for the contribution they would make to the winter scene, and it was evident that the promise of things to come in the garden was held by the faint colour of twigs and berries glimmering through the monochrome of snow and shadow. That, I think, is the real purpose of having 'winter interest': those faint reminders of springtime pleasures keep hope alive during a garden-maker's darkest hours.

Based loosely on the potential of the Wisconsin garden, this garden design makes a feature of winter-colouring roses as dividing hedges, foundation planting and massed foreground planting that emphasizes the natural woodland beyond the property line.

The garden can be seen at all times from the house; sliding glass doors

In this garden, the deck is raised to accommodate a slight gradient down towards the woodland boundary, and has an elevation of only a few feet which is screened by mass plantings of the species roses *Rosa pendulina* and *R. nitida*. Both are low growing, have good autumn foliage and hips, and the flowers of *nitida* have a curious lily-of-the-valley scent that is especially strong in the evening.

Along the side boundary, a row of red-twig lime (linden in the USA) trees terminates in a specimen tree of *Idesia polycarpa* that has fragrant acid-yellow flowers in summer followed by berries that hang in clusters like pendants of coral beads. The trees are underplanted with pools of early spring flowering bulbs, including the hardy *Cyclamen coum* 'Pewter Leaf' that has fuchsia-pink flowers above leaves so heavily variegated as to be nearly silver. Yellow winter aconites, *Eranthis hyemalis*, the palest lavender *Crocus tommasinianus* and the single snowdrops grow in drifts between the trees.

The corner formed by the other side boundary and the natural woods is filled in with several plants of *Picea pungens* 'Koster', a glaucous blue spruce that eventually grows to 2.5 m (8 ft). These are planted down the side, with a selection of species roses filling the corner and underplanted towards the front with *Rhododendron indicum* (*Azalea indica*) a semi-evergreen rhododendron with scarlet flowers in summer and fiery foliage in autumn, and a few plants of *Rhododendron luteum* towards the back. This also has a good autumn colouring and the toasted-brown seed pods hang on during winter; the clusters of fragrant yellow flowers in spring are good to have, too. *Hamamelis mollis* opens its clean-

A natural woodland setting provides an ideal showcase for massed plantings of simple single-flowered and species roses. These are often followed by brightly coloured autumn foliage and so continue to add to the garden picture beyond their flowering season.

lead onto a raised deck that is divided by a hedge of Rugosa roses from a small courtyard/utility area outside the kitchen door. This hedge is kept neatly trimmed to about 1.2 m (4 ft) high; the pruning is done in the spring so that the huge red hips and brightly coloured foliage are there to be enjoyed during the autumn and winter.

Raised decks are a comparatively easy way of dealing with uneven contours next to a house or sloping sites where the only other way of creating a level terrace for a seating area would entail earth-moving and grading. Thomas Church, the renowned American landscape architect, used decks to great effect. He called them 'wandering porches' and valued the illusion of spaciousness they provided in a garden. He especially appreciated that decks are 'at home among trees', and that constructing the deck around existing trees brought the built landscape into a closer relationship with the natural one.

A *Idesia polycarpa*
B *Tilia ruber*
C *Picea pungens* 'Koster'
D *Hamamelis mollis*
E *Viburnum × bodnantense*
F *Buxus sempervirens*
G *Viburnum × bodnantense* 'Dawn'
H *Rhododendron indicum*
I *R. luteum*
1 *Rosa pendulina*
2 *R. nitida*
3 *R. rugosa*
4 *R. virginiana*
5 *R. elegantula* 'Persetosa'
6 *R. glauca*
7 *R. setigera*
8 *R. sericea pteracantha*

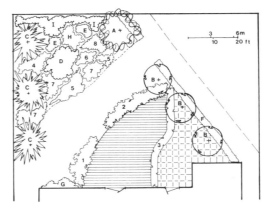

Plan for the Garden for All Seasons. By concealing boundary fences and graduating the height of the mixed shrub planting, the natural woods surrounding the garden (not shown in this plan) can be 'borrowed' and brought into the garden picture.

smelling flowers in early spring while the pink clusters of *Viburnun × bodnantense* have been enjoyed for some time.

The roses used include *R. virginiana*, that is upright growing to 1.5 m (5 ft) with bright green leaves setting off single pink flowers, followed by rich autumn colours and tiny ruby hips; *R. elegantula* 'Persetosa' (synonym *R. farreri persetosa*), *R. glauca*, and with *R. setigera* threading its ground-covering shoots through this mixed planting. *R. sericea pteracantha* is present for its startling stems, covered with broad ruby-red thorns.

Other plants, though not roses, which have good winter stems are *Cornus alba* 'Sibirica' with bright red branches, and *Salix alba vitellina* with glowing yellow stems. To ensure a good crop of these new growths, cut them hard back in early spring; they will then send up the brightly coloured shoots to colour the winter garden.

Add to this a bird-table and a hedgehog refuge to encourage wildlife into the garden (the berries and hips will probably be enough of an invitation), and the year-round garden is complete.

Left Clusters of tiny flagon-shaped hips on *R. moschata*, caught by the frost, look like sugared pastilles and add their charm to the winter garden.

Rose Gardening

Previous page In the close conditions of a well-stocked border pests and disease rapidly spread. Roses grown against walls are also especially prone to attack from mildew.

Below The planting hole must be large enough to accommodate the rootball without crowding, and deep enough to set the union between graft and rootstock 2.5 cm (1 in) below the soil surface.

Planting

One of the unwritten rules of gardening is that you must begin as you mean to carry on, and when it comes to planting this means taking care to do it properly as well as giving the plant the situation and soil it prefers. Fortunately, roses are easy subjects to deal with, generally preferring a sunny site in well-drained soil. Although roses will tolerate a wide range of pH values, a pH of 6.5 is best.

On the whole, roses prefer a clay soil that has been well dug with manure or has had compost added; superphosphate can be added at a rate of 120–175 g per 0.09 sq m (4–6 oz per sq yard). The site should be prepared several weeks before planting so that when the roses arrive they can be planted quickly. If you are not able to plant them immediately, plunge the roots in a bucket of peat or moist compost and cover the shoots with polythene bags to

keep them from dehydrating, a condition from which a bush rarely recovers.

There are roses which will grow in the shade of a north-facing wall and others, like the Rugosas, which will do well in sandy soil, but they, like their sisters need the same attention to planting.

Holes should be large enough to take the spread-out roots without crowding, about 45–60 cm (18–24 in) in diameter, and dug about one spade deep, about 30–37 cm (12–15 in). At planting time, loosen the bottom of the hole with the garden fork, stirring a handful of bonemeal and damp peat into the bottom of the hole. Add the same to the soil you have removed and mix it in well.

Inspect the roots of the bush before planting, snipping away any broken or diseased roots; do the same with the top growth. Most roses are grafted, so identify the bud-union, a knobby protuberance where the branches stem from the rootstock. Trim back any branches to about 25 cm (10 in) from the union. Spread the roots out in the bottom of the hole and replace half the soil, being sure to keep the plant upright. Give it a gentle shake to work the soil around the roots, then tread gently to firm the plant into the soil. Replace the rest of the soil and tread again.

While you are treading and firming, bear in mind that ideally you want the union to be about 2.5 cm (1 in) below the soil surface. This is very important: it helps to reduce suckering, where unwanted shoots sprout from the rootstock; helps to prevent the bush being rocked by strong winds; and protects the more tender union from possible frost damage. In the coldest climate zones, bury the union by at least 5 cm (2 in). Water the bush

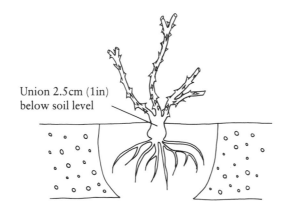

Union 2.5cm (1in)
below soil level

once to settle the soil then, when you have filled in with more soil, water a final time.

Roses should be planted during their dormant period, before they begin to show any sign of vegetative growth. This can be any time during winter or early spring, when the ground is workable and the change of season begins to wake the plant up.

The above directions apply to plants which are received bare-root from the nursery. But roses are also sold container-grown, and this is how they are most often found in garden centres. They will probably be in flower, and be more expensive. For preference, I would recommend that you buy bare-root plants from a reputable rose nursery. However, providing they are handled properly, container-grown roses will do. Basically, these bushes will not be deeply planted in their containers, so care should be taken to give them much more depth when planting out.

Soak the rose for several hours before planting (this will also make it easier to remove the container). Disturb the roots as little as possible. Plant as described above and water well and frequently until, in several weeks, they begin to send out fresh roots.

Pruning

Pruning ensures that roses produce good flower crops, healthy new growth to lengthen the plant's life and to keep it looking shapely and under control. While old roses do not require the ritual annual beheading of Hybrid Teas and Floribundas, the various groups require different pruning treatments.

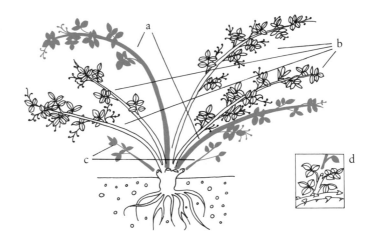

Generally, when pruning, endeavour to remove dead or diseased wood and spindly or twiggy growths as these will be unlikely to support a good crop of flowers. Crowded areas should also be thinned out.

Single-flowering Roses (Albas, Damasks, Gallicas and Centifolias) These should be pruned in the summer after flowering so that new flowering wood can establish itself that season, thus providing a good show of flowers the next year.

Repeat-flowering Roses (Hybrid Musks, Hybrid Perpetuals, Bourbons, Teas and Chinas) Prune during the winter. In warm regions, you can begin in November or December, while roses in colder zones should be left until February or March. Take out thin, twiggy wood, and on the Musks, Perpetuals and Bourbons cut back long shoots by one-third of their length. Rugosa roses, if grown as a hedge, should be lightly pruned in winter.

Prune ramblers and once-blooming climbers after they flower.
(a) Identify and remove the oldest flowering canes.
(b) Tie in sturdy new canes to the supports.
(c) Remove weak new growths and any surplus.
(d) Cut back laterals to four sets of leaves (inset).

Species, Sweetbriars and Burnets These are best if left to their own devices except when grown as a hedge. Sweetbriar hedges, for example, should have new growth tied in horizontally during the spring to establish the frame of the hedge and to encourage shoots to break along the length of the stems. In midsummer, cut back new growth to one-third of its length to make flowering spurs, or tie it in as necessary to fill in the hedge.

Climbing Roses (Clg. Hybrid Perpetuals, Clg. Teas, Noisettes and roses grown on pergolas, arches and pillars) These are the roses which are repeat- or continuously flowering on the wood produced in the same year and should be pruned during the winter when the plants are dormant. Begin by training the strong climbing shoots in as many directions as you can, tying them to the trellis or wires as near to the horizontal as possible, establishing a neat but natural-looking framework. The lateral shoots which break from these stems should be cut back to one-third of their length each year. This will form flower-bearing spurs, which are similarly pruned each year.

Ramblers (Hybrids of *R. wichuraiana*, *R. sempervirens*, *R. multiflora*, *R. arvensis*, *R. setigera*) These roses mostly flower only once on wood made the previous season and should be pruned immediately after flowering. They make long, supple wands that in one season can scramble into the topmost branches of a tree, or quickly cover the roof of a building. Train the first shoots in the desired direction and thereafter keep a watchful eye on them, cutting away any shoots seen snaking under roof tiles, coiling around guttering or threatening to engulf an adjacent garden feature or host tree. Old unproductive wood can be removed during winter.

Suckering and Dead-heading

Suckers, as mentioned earlier, are growths from the rootstock, which if not removed promptly can overtake the rose which has been grafted on. You can usually spot a sucker, if not a mile away, at least easily, since it will be markedly different from the top growth. The stem is sappier, perhaps with fewer or differently shaped thorns, the leaves will have a different texture and shape, and the colour of all three will be varied. Do not simply cut a sucker off; grab it firmly at the base and pull down sharply and away. This will remove the vestigial buds at its base. If you have not spotted it in time, dig down carefully around the base of the rose and cut it away

Prune repeat-flowering climbers during the dormant period.
(a) Remove all diseased, spent canes.
(b) Tie vigorous new canes to supports.
(c) Remove all the oldest canes and any weak new growth and suckers.
(d) Cut each flowering shoot back to two leaf buds (inset).

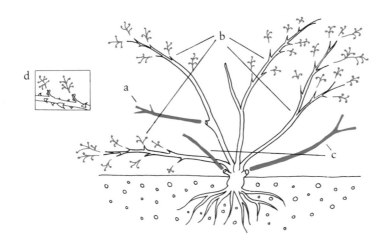

completely with a pruning knife.

Repeat-flowering roses are encouraged to keep up the show through the removal of spent flower heads, and those roses which hold their dead petals after flowering can be tidied by dead-heading. However, do not just drift through the garden pulling off faded petals: keep a pair of secateurs handy and, in the case of roses which produce their flowers singly, cut back to the first bud below the flower stalk, making the cut just above the leaf axil. Roses that produce flowers in sprays can be cut back more severely – pruned rather than dead-headed – to the third or fourth bud.

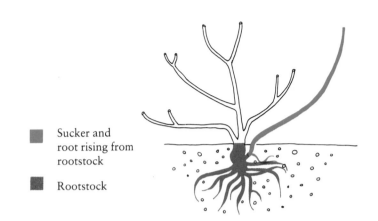

■ Sucker and root rising from rootstock

■ Rootstock

Pests

Bugs and fungi love old roses too, and in our fight against them we will be aided by good garden hygiene, fungicides and pesticides, either ecologically sound or high-tech. Keep gardens clear of rubbish, burning diseased wood and so on. Overcrowding of plants prevents the free flow of air and so encourages mildew and rust. It really does pay to 'Treat at the first sign of attack', so keep a watchful eye on the garden and a remedy at the ready.

Japanese beetles are small, brown and devastating, munching their way through leaves and flowers.

Caterpillars of various moths and flies cozy up in the leaves and developing flowers; foliage curls into neat tubes, edges are scalloped by scissoring jaws (late in the season when certain species are settling in for winter, whole bushes can be stripped of their foliage overnight) and flowers fail to develop.

Aphids, also known as green- or blackfly, latch onto young shoots to suck the sap, causing new growth to shrivel, stunt and die. Aphids are probably the most common pest, and it always surprises me how you can check a plant over one day and see nothing, and when you look again the next morning the stems are coated in bright green, faintly twitching clusters. One method of control, though not for the faint-hearted, is to pull the shoot through your finger tips, squeezing the aphids to pulp. The principle is the same as hanging a dead crow in a field to scare away any others that might consider landing. Otherwise, use a systemic spray that enters into the 'body' of the plant and is thus unavoidably consumed by the bugs as they feed.

Red spider mite is more resilient than the above, but is also a leaf sucker recognized by small yellow dots on foliage that grow into

Suckers are growths coming from the rootstock which if left will weaken the plant and eventually overtake it. They must be removed by either pulling them off with a sharp downwards tug, or by cutting away completely using a pruning knife to ensure that the buds at the base of the sucker are excised.

patches, followed by a haze of webbing on the underside of totally yellowed leaves. One friend swears by a strong solution of washing-up liquid sprayed routinely over suffering plants.

Diseases

Black spot appears as just that, black-brown blotches on leaves and stems, particularly, in my experience, on yellow-flowered roses. Eventually all the leaves drop off. Immediate spraying and keeping the ground beneath bushes clear of diseased foliage prevents the spread of the spores.

Rust affects leaves and stems and severe attacks can so debilitate the plant that it dies. Leaves begin to look speckled with white and then coral-coloured spots appear on the undersides, spreading to the stems which turn

Pegging the long whippy canes of taller growing shrub roses encourages flowering shoots to break along their length. The canes are held down by simple wire 'staples',

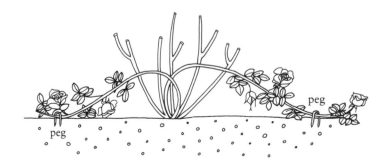

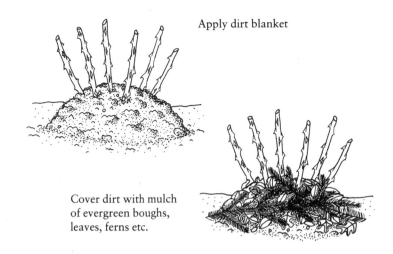

Apply dirt blanket

Cover dirt with mulch
of evergreen boughs,
leaves, ferns etc.

blotchy-brown. High-potash fertilizers can keep rust in check as can some sprays. Some hybrid Rugosas, like 'Rose à Parfum de l'Hay', are especially prone to it.

Mildew is the most common disease and, while not life-threatening, is unsightly. The leaves appear covered in a silvery powder and slightly shrivelled. 'Zéphirine Drouhin' is a martyr to mildew, but spraying with Bordeaux mixture from leaf bud, and then regularly throughout the season, helps. Roses grown against walls and in areas where air does not move freely are particularly susceptible to pest and disease, so pay special attention to their well-being.

There are any number of proprietary rose pesticides on the market that will deal with the whole gamut of rose perils. Often these contain quite strong chemicals, so care must be taken and the manufacturer's instructions adhered to for safety and to maximize benefit from the product.

Above In cold climates roses can be protected by a thick mulch of earth covered with a blanket of leaves, evergreen boughs, fern and so on. In spring this winterizing cover can be cleared away, dead top growth pruned and the rose fed to wake it from its winter hibernation. Climbers can be protected behind a curtain of sacking tacked over a blanket of straw, fern etc. But be sure to give their roots adequate cover too.

Left Parasitic rust is one of the most debilitating diseases to afflict roses.

Rose Recipes

China bowls brimming with fragrant rose petals, heads of lavender, powdered spices and scented herbs gathered at the peak of their savour, then carefully dried and blended with costly spices and perfumed oils, take pride of place in many homes. Positioned in a spot where the sun's rays can warm the mixture to release its scent on faint currents of air, the pot pourii adds to the ambient comfort of the best rooms.

There are two types of pot pourri, dry and moist; the term is French for 'rotten pot' as the original pot pourris were a sort of damp compost of blended petals and leaves seasoned with spices. This sort of pot pourri is kept in a closed jar or scent jar so that the mixture retains its moisture and remains fragrant longer than a dry blend.

In a moist pot pourri the original essential oils of the plants are present, more so than in a dry mixture, so the original flower scent is prevalent. Dry pot pourris, in which leaves and petals are crisp-dry, rely on the addition of scented oils to strengthen their perfume. The lid of a scent jar is removed to release the pot pourri fragrance while a dry pot pourri is kept in an open bowl, the more ornamental the better, and stirred occasionally to waken the scent.

Pot pourri is usually made from varied blends of flower petals and leaves, spices, essential oils, fixatives and salt. Rose petals, lavender and lemon verbena are the traditional main ingredients of most pot pourri recipes. Certain rose varieties hold their fragrance better than others when dried: 'Gloire de Guilan' and 'Kazanlik' are Damask roses grown in the Near East to make attar of roses; the old *Rosa gallica officinalis*, the Apothecary's Rose, has deep red, highly scented flowers; 'Mme Isaac Pereire' and the thornless rose 'Zéphirine Drouhin', both Bourbons, keep their distinct perfume of crushed raspberries when dry.

Generally the roses for pot pourri are pink or red, although white petals can also be used. However, these dry to look like scraps of yellowed paper and so are not such an attractive addition.

The old-fashioned English lavender traditionally provided its spicy mauve flowers to pot pourri, but it grows to quite a large scraggy bush. Dwarf varieties like 'Munstead' or 'Hidcote' are more manageable in the

Right Put bowls of pot pourri in a sunny window; the warmth releases the fragrance.

Far right 'Kazanlik' has been used for generations to make attar of roses.

garden and are good companions, planted as a border, to a bed of old roses; their flowers are richly coloured and just as highly scented as the old-fashioned sort.

The somewhat tender shrub, *Aloysia triphylla* (synonym *Lippia citriodora*), or lemon verbena, is a true joy for its long crinkly leaves smell strongly of lemon and keep their scent well when dried. Other leaves to be added are any of the herbs, sage, rosemary, santolina, thyme, curry plant, marjoram, bay and of course the scented leaf geraniums which give a wide choice of fragrance from lemon to a rich chocolate scent; even walnut leaves can be used for their pleasant fruity perfume.

Pinks, violets, pot marigolds, heliotrope, lily-of-the-valley and meadowsweet are just a few of the fragrant flowers that will add perfume and colour to pot pourri bowls. Cloves, nutmeg, cinnamon and allspice are the powdered spices most often added to enrich the scent of pot pourri blends. Exotic spices like coriander, mace and cardamon can also be used to heighten the fragrance.

The essential oils used are mostly floral in origin (rose oil is especially favoured), although ones derived from exotic woods and resins, such as patchouli and sandalwood, are used to strengthen the scent of the pot pourri and to give it a pronounced character such as woody, citrus, rose, and so on. Essential oils are also used in blends to freshen a 'stale' pot-pourri – one that has been sitting out for some time and has lost much of its original perfume.

Some flower petals and leaves hold their scent well when dried, but with others, like jasmine, the scent is more fugitive and so the flowers must be helped to hold their perfume. This is done by blending the petals with scented powder derived from plant roots and resins. The chief one used is orris root powder, which is derived from the dried root of the Florentine iris and smells faintly of violets. Gum benzoin, patchouli leaves, sandalwood shavings and vanilla-scented tonka beans are also used.

Salt is used to 'pickle' the leaves and petals, and in old recipes the sort called for is usually 'basalt' or 'bay salt'. This is thought to refer to sea salt of the coarse gravelly kind that can be easily obtained from health-food shops and most supermarkets.

The best time to gather flowers for pot pourri is in the morning when the dew has dried from the petals, but before the sun has warmed them too much. Select only the flowers that are in their prime and pull them apart carefully so that they do not bruise. That is the counsel of perfection. I have found, however, that the petals I gather from rose blossoms which are about to drop, are just as sweetly scented. These I collect and simply scatter over the top of my bowl of vintage pot pourri. Whole flower heads are treated in the same manner and dry perfectly. Nevertheless, when you are making the initial batch of pot pourri, it is just as well to take the time to do it properly.

Petals and leaves must be dried slowly, spread flat in a single layer in a place that is cool, dark and ventilated; under the bed or a chest of drawers are good spots. Small amounts of petals can be dried spread out over rush floor-mats, in shallow cardboard boxes, or on newspaper. But if you plan to produce masses of pot pourri, take the time to make net drying-racks that can be stacked in a cool corner.

The soft violet of English lavender and the warm pink rambling rose 'American Pillar' make a tasteful display at the restored Gertrude Jekyll garden, Hestercombe, Somerset. Lavender is an essential pot pourri ingredient. Scentless roses, like 'American Pillar' are nevertheless valuable since their rich colouring adds to the visual pleasure of a well-mixed pot pourri.

Make a wooden frame from 5 × 2.5 cm wood; the overall dimensions will be determined by the size of the area where they will be stacked. Artists' canvas stretchers, available from art supply shops, offer a ready-made alternative. Stretch sheer curtain netting or butter muslin over the frame and nail short legs at each corner.

Lavender, thyme and other small flowers and leaves can be dried on the stalk. Gather lavender with long stems then tie these in small bundles and hang them upside-down in a cool airy spot out of direct sunlight. When they are dry, simply crumble the flowers and leaves from the stalks onto a sheet of newspaper.

It is important that the pot pourri looks as good as it smells, so you should include some whole flower heads and entire leaves to produce a contrast of colour and shape. These may be chosen simply for their appearance rather than scent, like love-in-the-mist and delphinium flowers, or you can use entire perfect rose buds or marigold flowers. To dry them whole you simply lay them individually on a bed of dry silver sand, or on silica gel, which is considerably more expensive, spread evenly in the bottom of a shallow box. Take care that they do not overlap, and then cover them with a layer of sand or gel. Put them in a warm place for several days and they will emerge with their colour and shape intact.

Orange and lemon peel, scraped with a zester to make fine threads without including any of the pith, can be dried slowly on sheets of greaseproof paper (muslin or plain paper would absorb the essential oil) to make a pleasing addition to the pot pourri.

No special tools are needed to make pot pourri, although a large jar or crock with a close-fitting lid should be obtained before you begin as the pot pourri must be kept for some weeks in such a pot to allow the perfumes to merge and mature. Do not use plastic or metal containers; only glass or crockery will do.

For measuring you will need kitchen scales, measuring jug and spoons and a calibrated pipette, or eye-dropper, for measuring out drops of essential oil.

Blend the spices and fixatives in a glass bowl and try if possible to purchase whole spices to grind yourself, since freshly ground spice has a far better scent than pre-ground package spice.

Finally, use pot pourri recipes simply as a starting point, adjusting the quantities and blends to suit your materials and your own nose. Keep a note of what you do so that you will be able to recreate a really successful blend – that is how the earliest recipes have reached us, through the gentlewoman at work in her stillroom noting the flowers and spices, quantities and methods of her pot pourris to pass on within her family.

Edwardian Pot Pourri

This recipe was provided by Violet, Duchess of Rutland, one of the great beauties of the Edwardian period, to Dorothy Allhusen for her *Book of Scents and Dishes*, published in 1926. By 'rose leaves' the Duchess means 'rose petals'.

'When the roses are ready for gathering pluck off the petals. Dry in the sun or in a warm place on sheets of paper. When quite dry put them in a box. As soon as the sweet herbs are ready to pick, take about as many as the rose-leaves, cut into rather small pieces,

Whole flower heads, like these rose buds, add to the texture of pot pourri, and can be dried in boxes of silver sand. But once a bowl of pot pourri is complete, it is possible to add entire flowers by simply tossing them onto the top of the mix; the salt and spices it contains will still do their jobs, and the flower colour and shape will be retained just as well.

and dry them in the same manner. When these are quite dry, salt the rose-leaves with a handful or two of common salt. Let them dry for a day or two. Then add the herbs, with a few pieces of bay salt in very small lumps, and some pot pourri powder [orris root]. It is then ready to put into bowls.'

Lady Betty Germaine Pot Pourri of 1750

From the same book comes Vita Sackville-West's recipe for the pot pourri she knew from Knole. This is my adaptation:

Dry for a day or two, violets, rose petals, lavender, myrtle flowers, verbena, rosemary, lemon balm and scented geranium. Put into a glazed jar with a close-fitting lid. Cut a piece of card to the exact size of the jar and keep it pressed down on the flowers. Add a handful of salt for the flowers. Add more petals, leaves and salt until the jar is full. Stir before each new addition. When the jar is full add a spice mix made from plenty of cinnamon, mace, nutmeg, pepper and dried lemon peel. For a large jar add: 250 g (8 oz, 1 cup) orris root powder, 30 g (1 oz) storax, 30 g (1 oz) gum benzoin, 60 g (2 oz, $\frac{1}{4}$ cup) powdered root of *Acorus calamus* (sweet sedge), a few drops of musk and $\frac{1}{2}$ teaspoon rose essence. 'Mix all well together, press it down well and spread bay salt on top to exclude the air until the January or February following. Keep the jar in a cool dry place.'

Rose and Lavender Dry Pot Pourri
This is a very simple recipe
with a fresh clean scent.

300 g (10 oz, 1¼ cups) rose petals
90 g (3 oz, ½ cup) lavender flowers
90 g (3 oz, ½ cup) lemon verbena
60 g (2 oz, ¼ cup) orris root powder
1 teaspoon each allspice, cinnamon,
cloves and nutmeg
rose essence

Blend the dried flower petals and leaves together. Mix the orris root powder with the spices and add to the flower petals. Stir gently and put into a crock. Add 10–12 drops of rose essence, the amount used will depend on the strength of the rose petals' perfume. Fit the lid and leave for up to two weeks to mature, stirring occasionally.

Simple Moist Pot Pourri

250 g (8 oz, 1 cup) rose petals
150 g (5 oz, ½ cup) each bay salt
and table salt
1 large handful lavender flowers, herbs to choice and scented geranium leaves
1 teaspoon ginger
½ teaspoon cloves
30 g (1 oz) orris root powder

Dry the rose petals for two days. Mix the salts together and add to the petals in a jar in alternate layers. Leave to cure for ten days, stirring daily after the fifth day. Then add the remaining ingredients and mix well. Cover the jar tightly and leave to mature for several weeks.

Edible flowers are back in fashion, and rose petals, besides being preserved (by painting them with beaten egg white, then dusting them with powdered sugar and leaving them to dry on a wire rack), or scattered fresh among salad leaves, can be a delicious ingredient in syrups and jams, from which wonderful summer deserts can be fashioned.

Rose Syrup

250 g (8 oz, 1 cup) freshly gathered petals
of a highly scented rose like
Rosa gallica officinalis
Granulated sugar

Put the petals into a stainless steel saucepan, pressing them down gently. Barely cover with cold water, adding 250 ml (8 fl oz, 1 cup) at a time. Bring to the boil. Remove from the heat and for every measure of water add 750 g (1½ lbs, 3 cups) of sugar. Stir gently to blend and then return to the boil. Reduce the heat and simmer slowly until the mixture becomes syrupy. Stir occasionally and gently. Strain through muslin or a jelly bag into clean jars. Seal and leave in a warm place for at least one week before using.

Rose Snow
Having made the above syrup you can now make this fanciful desert.

1 package of unflavoured powdered gelatin
120 ml (4 fl oz, ½ cup) cold water
250 ml (8 fl oz, 1 cup) rose syrup
Pinch of salt
2 large egg whites

Far right One of the oldest roses and the one most frequently used by our ancestors for preparing rose confections is *Rosa gallica officinalis*, commonly known as the Apothecary's Rose.

Mix the gelatin and water and dissolve over a pan of boiling water. Add the rose syrup and salt and stir until the salt is dissolved. Chill until the mixture begins to set, at which time add the egg whites. Beat well until the mixture holds its shape. Put a layer of puréed raspberries into the bottom of four glass bowls and then spoon in drifts of rose snow. Decorate with preserved petals, or use fresh one.

Rose Petal Jam

500 g (1 lb, 2 cups) rose petals
750 g (1½ lbs, 3 cups) granulated sugar
2 tablespoons of honey
1 teaspoon lemon juice

The roses must be freshly gathered and only the best petals used. Snip away the white from the base of each petal and cut the petals into several pieces. Put the petals in a stainless steel saucepan and add the boiling water. Return to the boil, then reduce the heat and simmer until the petals are tender. Strain into a clean saucepan, reserving the petal pulp. Add the sugar and honey to the strained liquid and simmer until it becomes quite syrupy. Stir in the petal pulp and simmer for forty minutes. Add the lemon juice and simmer for at least another thirty minutes. Pour into sterilized jars (this quantity is enough for two small jars). Cover and seal in a bain-marie for ten minutes.

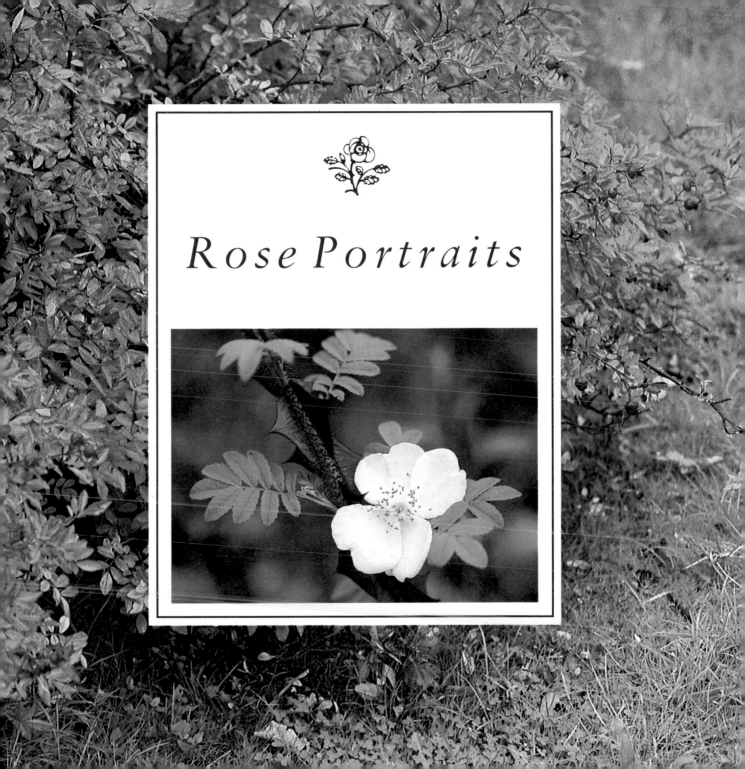

Rose Portraits

'Abraham Darby'

'Alfred de Dalmas'
(synonym 'Mousseline')
Moss rose, with dainty, pearly-pink, semi-double flowers that are very sweetly scented. The moss is touched with pink fading to russet as it ages. The shrub is small, 90 × 60 cm (3 × 2 ft), and has a very tidy habit making it suitable for container gardens. It flowers continuously throughout summer and will often carry on well in autumn. 1855.

'Amy Robsart'
Sweetbriar rose, with shocking pink flowers that cover the bush briefly during summer. It is extremely vigorous, sending up sturdy shoots to 3.8 m (12 ft), and so can be used to make an impressive hedge. In my garden this form has the most fragrant apple-scented foliage, while its sister, 'Magnifica', although less fragrant, is half the size and twice as floriferous, being blanketed in summer with semi-double, cherry-red flowers that fade to dusty pink. 1894.

'Abraham Darby'
English Rose, with yellow- and apricot-shaded flowers shaped like huge, round goblets that bloom throughout the season from early spring. Large glossy, disease-resistant foliage on a bushy shrub. 1.5 × 1.5 m (5 × 5 ft). 1985.

'Albéric Barbier'
Rambler, with good, glossy green, healthy foliage and creamy-white flowers scented of apples. It has one major burst of flowers in summer but this is often followed by quite a few blooms throughout the season. It will tolerate shade and so can be grown to brighten a north-facing wall. To 4.5 m (15 ft). 1900.

'Baron Girod de l'Ain'

'Assemblage des Beautés'
Gallica, also known as 'Rouge Eblou-issante', with an abundance of well-perfumed, neatly double, clear crimson flowers that fade to purple with age. It flowers once in summer on a tidy bush. 90 × 90 cm (3 × 3 ft). 1823.

'Baron Girod de l'Ain'
Hybrid Perpetual, with very double, deeply cupped, cherry-red flowers that are richly scented. Curiously, each petal has a ragged edge which is made more pronounced by its whiteness. The shrub is sturdy, upright to 1.5 m (5 ft), repeat-flowering, and the flowers are borne in clusters. 1897.

'Baronne Adolphe de Rothschild'
(synonym 'Baroness Rothschild')
Hybrid Perpetual, with large, cupped, clear pink flowers on a healthy, hardy shrub to 1.5 m (5 ft). The flowers are very fragrant and repeat throughout the season. 1868.

'Belle de Crécy'
Gallica, with rich, wine-red, highly scented flowers that appear once over a long summer season. The flowers are extremely double, with hundreds of petals crowded around a tiny green 'eye', and carried on almost thornless, upright stems. It makes a small neat bush, 1.2 m × 90 cm (4 × 3 ft), and can be grown in a container or to make a neat hedge. Known since 1829.

'Blairii No. 2'

'Belle Story'
English Rose, with large, pale pink, fragrant flowers. When fully open the petals fall back from the brilliant golden boss of stamens so that the flowers look somewhat like a peony. It makes a bushy shrub only 1.2 × 1.2 m (4 × 4 ft); an ideal size for a small garden or terrace. 1984.

'The Bishop'
Centifolia × Gallica, which has flowers that are richly tinted with a mix of purple, cherry-red and burgundy, and sweetly perfumed. They are fully double and appear only in early summer on a small upright shrub, 1.2 m × 90 cm (4 × 3 ft). Unknown origin and date.

'Blairii No. 2'
Climbing Bourbon with curvaceous, double, pale pink flowers that shade to deep blush-pink at their centres. Pleasingly scented, it is vigorous enough to climb into small trees or to train in tripods in the flower border. Repeat-flowering, and in a good year it will produce a staggering number of blooms. It grows to 3.5 m (12 ft). 1845.

'Blush Noisette'
(synonym 'Noisette Carnée')
Noisette, producing clusters of pinky-mauve flowers that are semi-double around pronounced gold stamens. It is well-scented and its growth is refined, making a loose, healthy bush up to 2.5 m (8 ft). It can be trained as a climber and will tolerate shade and a north-facing aspect. This was one of the first Noisettes, introduced 1817.

'Boule de Neige'
Bourbon, with richly scented, creamy-white flowers flushed with pink that appear in clusters continuously from midsummer through autumn. The slenderness of the branches and the shiny green foliage add to its beauty. It grows to 1.2 m × 90 cm (4 × 3 ft) and can be used for container gardens. 1867.

'Bredon'
English Rose, with buff-yellow flowers that have a pleasant fruity scent. A small sturdy bush to 90 × 60 cm (3 × 2 ft), it flowers continuously and is ideal for a terrace garden. 1984.

'Buff Beauty'

'Buff Beauty'

Hybrid Musk, with large trusses of apricot-yellow flowers on smooth stems. The foliage is glossy and dark green, and the shrub is vigorous and spreading to 1.5 × 1.2 m (5 × 4 ft). Very strongly scented, it flowers continuously and will tolerate a site in shade. 1939.

'Cardinal de Richelieu'

Gallica, with luxurious velvety flowers, which are a particularly deep shade of purple and sweetly perfumed. They appear only in summer in clusters on a tidy shrub that is well-furnished with glossy, dark green foliage. Another good hedging Gallica, to 1.2 m × 90 cm (4 × 3 ft). It responds to extra attention, so feed it well and prune judiciously. *c*. 1840.

'Céline Forestier'

Noisette, with primrose-yellow flowers, flushed pink and a sweet, strong scent. The flowers are large for the group and very double, appearing continuously on a small climber, to 1.8 m (6 ft), of graceful vigorous habit. 1842.

'Climbing Cécile Brunner'

Polyantha-type, this and its bush form are commonly called the Sweetheart Rose or the Buttonhole Rose on account of the diminutive flowers; each bud is only the size of a thumbnail and the blush-pink flowers are equally dainty. Where the bush is reluctant to grow the climber romps away to 7.5 m (25 ft). The foliage is glossy and healthy and the gently perfumed flowers appear continuously over a long season. It will tolerate shade. 1894.

'Complicata'

'Climbing Cécile Brunner'

'Climbing Mme Caroline Testout'

Hybrid Tea, with bold ruffled flowers of softest pink that are wonderfully scented. It blooms once, lavishly, in early summer, followed by fewer flowers over the remainder of the season. A sturdy rose, it makes canes up to 3 m (10 ft) with stout, leathery leaves. This is a climbing Hybrid Tea rose, but its great beauty won it a place in this list and my garden, and it is one of the earliest HT roses, from 1901.

'Complicata'

Gallica, with single, vibrant pink flowers with pale centres around a large gold boss of stamens. It has a good scent and attractive grey-green foliage. The shrub is vigorous and will grow to 3 m (10 ft) if used as a climber; it looks especially beautiful if grown into a small tree. Otherwise, grow it as a specimen shrub or trained against a pillar. It flowers once during summer. Unknown date and origin.

'Comte de Chambord'

'The Countryman'
English Rose, with clear pink flowers with a strong fragrance. Makes a low spreading shrub to 90 cm × 1 m (3 × 3.5 ft). Has two main flowerings with intermittent flowers in-between. 1987.

'Desprez à Fleur Jaune'
Noisette, with wonderful blushing-pink flowers touched with gold that have an unusual fruity scent, like ripe plums. It grows vigorously to 6 m (20 ft), making it a good choice for training into trees; it will also tolerate shade. 1830.

'Duchesse de Brabant'
Tea rose, with very double flowers, shell-pink shading darker to the centre. Very fragrant and flowering continuously, like all Tea roses, it needs a sunny sheltered spot to give of its best. It is an upright shrub, from 1–1.5 m (3–5 ft). This was President Roosevelt's favourite rose. 1857.

'English Garden'
English Rose, with fully double flowers of soft apricot-yellow that open flat to reveal their true 'old-fashioned' style. Only slightly fragrant, but the neat shape and petite size, 1 m × 75 cm (3 × 2.5 ft) makes it a must for the terrace or small garden. 1986.

'Comte de Chambord'
Portland rose, with very double, deep pink flowers that are richly scented. For a shrub only 90 × 60 cm (3 × 2 ft) the grey-green foliage and flowers appear oversized. It flowers continuously and generously. 1863.

'Cornelia'
Hybrid Musk, with trusses of tiny, coppery-pink flowers that have a delicate perfume. The foliage reflects the copper colouring and the smooth stems have a definite red colour so that the shrub is particularly effective in the autumn border. It grows to about 1.5 × 1.5 m (5 × 5 ft) and flowers continuously. 1925.

'Cornelia'

'Fair Bianca'
English Rose, similar in colour and shape to the pure white Damask, 'Mme Hardy'. It has a good fragrance and a tidy upright habit, to 1 m × 60 cm (3 × 2 ft), so it is ideal for the terrace or small gardens. 1982.

'The Fairy'
Polyantha, a multi-flowered, blush-pink rose that has a good procumbent habit so is much used for ground-cover and to grow in containers on terraces. To 60 cm × 1.2 m (2 × 4 ft). Little fragrance, but it flowers continuously over a long season. 1932.

'Fantin-Latour'
Centifolia, with clusters of double, pink flowers of a delicate hue and sweet scent. It is a large spreading shrub, to 1.5 × 1.2 m (5 × 4 ft), that flowers once in summer. Named for the artist renowned for his flower portraits.

'Félicité Perpétue'
Rambler, with abundant clusters of tiny, pearl-white flowers that are slightly scented. It is considered evergreen as it will hold its leathery green leaves during winter, but the flowers appear only once during summer. A very vigorous rose, it will smother the support in long sinuous branches up to 6 m (20 ft) long. Wonderful for clothing tall trees, growing against a north wall, in shade or in damp places. An amenable rose. 1827.

'The Fairy'

'Ferdinand Pichard'

'Ferdinand Pichard'

Hybrid Perpetual, with flowers boldly striped and splashed raspberry and white. Very sweetly scented of raspberries, too. It makes an upright shrub, 1.5 × 1.2 m (5 × 4 ft), with sturdy canes that bend earthwards under the weight of blossoms breaking along their length. After the first mad flush of flowers, slightly fewer recur during the rest of the season. 1921.

'Fimbriata'

Rugosa, the flowers look just like the old cottage garden pinks as the edges of the petals are prettily serrated. They are small, double, shell-pink and sweetly scented. It makes a small bush with neat upright habit to 1.2 × 1.2 m (4 × 4 ft). Like other Rugosas, the foliage has good autumn colour and since it does not mind the shade can be used in the foreground of woodland plantings. 1891.

'François Juranville'

Rambler, flowering once on long whippy shoots, the flowers are large, fully double and peachy-pink. They appear just once in summer, but compensate with a good scent. The shiny green foliage is copper burnished so that this rose is sometimes mistaken for the very popular 'Albertine'. It will grow against north walls or can be used for a fairly thornless groundcover. Up to 4.5 m (15 ft). 1906.

'Fru Dagmar Hastrup'
(synonym 'Frau Dagmar Hartopp')

Rugosa, with highly fragrant, single, pearly-pink flowers. In autumn the flowers give way to ruby-red hips the size of muscat grapes, nestling in the brightly coloured foliage. Makes a spreading bush 90 cm × 1.2 m (3 × 4 ft). 1914.

'Fru Dagmar Hastrup'

'The Garland'

'The Garland'

Musk rose, that was Gertrude Jekyll's favourite climber and rightly so. It is vigorous, to 4.5 m (15 ft), and offers a sheet of strongly perfumed, flower clusters during summer. It has dainty foliage to match the single white flowers, and it will grow in shade and near water. 1835.

'Georg Arends'

Hybrid Perpetual, with big, blowsy, clear pink flowers. The fragrance is strong and so is the shrub, making an upright bush to 1.5 × 1.2 m (5 × 4 ft), that flowers freely and continuously. 1910.

'Général Kléber'

Moss rose, with pearl-pink, sweetly scented flowers that appear once in summer. Makes a good upright shrub to 1.5 × 1.2 m (5 × 4 ft). Commemorates Napoleon's chief-of-staff in Egypt, who in 1800 was assassinated in Cairo. 1856.

'Gertrude Jekyll'

English Rose, with large, extremely scented, rich pink flowers that begin as tightly rolled buds; this rose is now being used to make the first commercial rose essence in over 200 years. Makes a tall, upright shrub for the back of the border. To 1.2 × 1 m (4 × 3 ft). 1986.

'Gloire de Dijon'

Tea rose, a climber with golden, apricot-yellow flowers tinted pink at the centre. They look like crumpled silk hankies and have the delicious 'tea-rose' scent so evocative of old-fashioned gardens. My favourite rose, it begins early in the summer and, during mild winters, has carried on blooming into December. The shiny green foliage is prone to black spot and wet weather turns the flowers to mush, but it is a 'must have' in spite of these failings. Appreciates a warm sunny wall. To 3.5 m (12 ft). 1853.

'Gloire de France'

Gallica, with masses of very double, shell-pink flowers that are very sweetly scented. It flowers only once, but does so with a vengeance. The foliage is clear green and healthy, and the new growth begins upright, but collapses under the weight of blossoms, so either give it support or room to spread. To 1.4 × 1.5 m (4 × 5 ft). 1819.

'Gloire de Guilan'

Damask rose, with shell-pink, very double, highly-scented flowers produced freely in early summer. The stems are fairly whippy, so without the support of a tripod or other framework it falls about. Collected in the Middle East in 1949 by Nancy Lindsay, she described its qualities perfectly: 'The attar-of-roses rose of Guilan and Manzanderan grows in yard-high thickets of almond-green decorated with ambrosial flowers of translucent celestial pink.'

'Graham Thomas'

English Rose, with rich, pure yellow flowers that have a strong Tea rose perfume. It blooms continuously on a vigorous bush; the foliage is soft, green and shiny. Named for the influential English rosarian and author of several authoritative books on old roses, Mr Thomas was instrumental in re-establishing the garden worthiness of old-fashioned shrub roses. To 1.2 × 1.2 m (4 × 4 ft). 1983.

'Graham Thomas'

'Great Maiden's Blush'

'Great Maiden's Blush' (synonym Cuisse de Nymphe)

Alba, with shell-pink flowers nestling amidst the grey-green foliage. They are very sweetly scented and appear in abundance during summer. It makes a large, spreading shrub up to 1.5 × 1.5 m (5 × 5 ft) that will grow well in the shade of a woodland planting; it can also be used for hedging. This is one of the oldest garden roses in cultivation, known since the fifteenth century.

'Gruss an Teplitz'

Bourbon, with wine-red, fully double flowers in clusters that have an especially strong fruity scent, like peaches spiked with cloves. The first flowering is profuse followed with a good repeat. The shrub is large and spreading to 2 × 1.5 m (7 × 5 ft) and can be used for hedges or trained against a low support. Prettily rounded leaves, but inclined to mildew. 1897.

'Henri Martin'

Moss, with clusters of semi-double, crimson flowers, sweetly scented and appearing in their hundreds on long canes to 2 m (7 ft). It will do well against a north wall. The stems are lightly mossed and it flowers once during summer. 1863.

'Heritage'

English Rose, with medium-sized, cup-shaped flowers, soft pink and with a strong citrus scent. It flowers continuously throughout the season on a sturdy bush to 1.2 × 1.2 m (4 × 4 ft). 1984.

'Hermosa'

China, with small, goblet-shaped flowers, sweetly fragrant and a delicate raspberry pink. This is not a robust rose, and grows only to 90 × 30 cm (35 × 12 in). It is susceptible to winter frosts, so it enjoys the coddling which container growing in a sheltered position can offer. Plant several in a Versailles tub to good effect. 1840.

'Ispahan'

Damask, extremely fragrant, double, clear pink flowers on an upright bush to 1.2 × 1 m (4 × 3 ft). The flowers appear in midsummer and continue longer than most of the other roses in the group. Before 1832.

'Kazanlik'

Damask, grown for its rich, ambrosial fragrance to produce attar of roses. The tender pink flower petals are like gossamer silk and when dried are an

'Ispahan'

'Königin von Dänemark'

'Lady Penzance'
Sweetbriar, with small russet-pink flowers going to gold at the centre around a bright crown of stamens. They appear rather sparsely on a spreading bush to 1.8 × 1.8 m (6 × 6 ft). The foliage has the characteristic apple scent, some say it is the most fragrant, but in my garden it is only moderately so. The flowers are followed by small, burnished-red hips. 1894.

'La Noblesse'
Centifolia, with extremely fragrant, silvery-pink flowers like a many layered silken ruff. The shrub has a neat habit and is small for the group, up to 1.2 × 1.2 m (4 × 4 ft). It flowers profusely in the summer only. 1856.

'Lawrence Johnston'
Climber, with large, semi-double vibrant yellow flowers that appear very early in spring and carry on for a surprisingly long time. It is subtly fragrant, with a hint of lemons, and very vigorous, sending out strong canes to 7.5 m (20 ft). Named for the son of an expatriate American family, he made one of England's most famous influential gardens, Hidcote Manor in Gloucestershire. 1923.

'Louis Gimard'
Moss, with rich, lavender-pink flowers that pale toward the outer petals to soft pink. They are extremely fragrant and very double. The abun-

essential pot pourri ingredient. It makes a large vigorous shrub to 1.5 × 1.2 m (5 × 4 ft) that can be grown in a shady spot. It has just one delicious summer flowering. An ancient rose from the Middle East.

'Königin von Dänemark'
Alba, with smallish flowers in summer, shell-pink deepening toward the centre and wonderfully fragrant. They are very double; the petals crowd around a protruding green eye set like

a coronet at the centre of each flower. The glaucous foliage is coarse and the habit lax, up to 1.5 × 1.2 m (5 × 4 ft). It will tolerate shade. 1826.

'La Belle Distinguée'
Sweetbriar, with clusters of tiny, double, burgundy-red flowers on a demure bush that grows slowly to 1.5 × 1.2 m (5 × 4 ft). The foliage is tight and dark, and probably has the least fragrant leaves of all the sweetbriars. Date unknown.

'Louise Odier'

dant moss is dark and tinged with purple, the stems are very prickly on a small bush to 1.2 m × 90 cm (4 × 3 ft). It flowers once in the summer. 1877.

'Louise Odier'
Bourbon, with delicate, sugar-almond pink flowers, blushing raspberry when first opened. It is hard to credit that such a delicate bloom could have such a powerful scent. It makes a sturdy upright shrub to 1.5 × 1.2 m (5 × 4 ft) and flowers continuously, well into the autumn. 1851.

'Mme Alfred Carrière'
Noisette, with clusters of large double flowers seemingly carved from ivory, and richly perfumed. It flowers continuously, and is a vigorous and healthy climber up to 3.8 m (12 ft) well-furnished with large mid-green foliage. It can be trained into trees, or against a north wall. 1879.

'Mme Grégoire Staechelin'
Climbing Hybrid Tea of exceptional beauty, with large, soft pink flowers. The reverse of the petals are a darker tint so the blossoms are beautifully modelled. Strong growing to 4.5 m (15 ft), it flowers only once. 1927.

'Mme Hardy'
Damask, with pure white flowers that have a rich, strong perfume. The blooms are quite large for the group, very double, with the central petals folding in toward the pronounced

green 'eye'. It makes an attractive upright shrub to 1.5 × 1.5 m (5 × 5 ft) with sturdy foliage that is almost as sharp a green as a parrot. It flowers once, but profusely, in summer. 1832.

'Mme Isaac Pereire'

Bourbon, a sumptuous rose with lush magenta-red flowers as big as a hand; the scent is extraordinarily rich and fruity. Thankfully it flowers repeatedly, so one may never be without it, and it is astonishing to watch the tight little buds explode with such extravagant results. She is quite statuesque to 1.8 × 1.5 m (6 × 5 ft) and robust. 1881.

'Mme Legras de St Germain'

Alba, the centres of the small white flowers are tinted ivory. Strongly scented and almost thornless, the soft glaucous foliage complements the flowers prettily. It makes a tall shrub up to 2 m (7 ft), or can be grown with support as a climber to make double that. It flowers only once and will tolerate shade, so is useful for brightening a dark corner. Since 1848.

'Mme Pierre Oger'

Bourbon, with delicate white flowers; the tips of each petal blush raspberry-pink. It flowers continously. The blossoms are small and fragile looking, but pack a highly scented punch, much like its sister 'Louise Odier'. It makes a slender shrub to 1.2 × 1.2 m (4 × 4 ft) and will grow in a container. 1878.

'Mme Pierre Oger'

'Mme Plantier'

Alba, with fully double, clear white flowers that are very richly perfumed. Makes a lax spreading shrub to 1.5 m (5 ft), or can be trained into a tree or up another support as a low climber to 4 m (12 ft). Flowers only once but is an extremely elegant, hardy rose that will grow in the shade. 1835.

'Magnifica'

Sweetbriar, and the best for flowers. In the summer it is encased in clusters of flowers that open the colour of a cardinal's hat and fade slowly to silvery-pink. At their centre is a coronet of golden stamens. All this show is to compensate for the middling scent of the dense green foliage, but if I could have only one sweetbriar this would be it. Makes a superb hedge, to 1.5 × 1.2 m (5 × 4 ft). 1916.

'Mermaid'

Climbing, with broad, clear yellow, single flowers that deepen in colour around the big central boss of stamens. Vigorous, up to 10 m (30 ft), and continuously covered with lightly scented blossoms. It has good, shiny green foliage and will grow against a north wall. 1918.

'Mermaid'

'Nathalie Nypels'
Polyantha, with clusters of apricot-pink flowers on a bushy, spreading plant that can be used as ground-cover if planted closely together, to 90 × 90 cm (3 × 3 ft). This rose featured in many of Gertrude Jekyll's garden schemes. This is really a Floribunda, but again beauty and its abundant autumn-flowering have qualified it as well as age. 1919.

'Nozomi'
Procumbent, with tiny silvery-pink flowers set in russet-tinted, shiny green foliage. It makes a dense, spreading mat 60 cm × 1.8 m (2 × 6 ft). This is a modern rose, introduced in 1968, and included because it is so very useful for garden making. Use it to cascade over retaining walls, as a carpet for bulbs to push through or below small shrubs of more upright habit. 1968.

'Othello'
English Rose, with large double flowers, strongly scented and velvety dark-crimson that fades to soft shades of mauve and purple. This is a sturdy bush with lush foliage, but only 1.4 m × 90 cm (4 × 3 ft). 1986.

'Perdita'
English Rose, with blushing apricot-pink flowers, very double and richly fragrant; it won the 1984 prize for scent from the Royal National Rose Society. Makes a strong, bushy, small shrub to 1.2 m × 90 cm (4 × 3 ft) and

flowers repeatedly through the season.
1983.

'Perle d'Or'
Polyantha, with clusters of creamy-buff flowers set in shiny, deep green foliage. Very like 'Cécile Brunner', and mildly fragrant. Makes a dense, some-what tender, continuously flowering shrub that can be trained as a low climber against a warm wall. To 1.5 m (5 ft). 1884.

'Petite de Hollande'
Centifolia, bearing many clusters of small, double, clear pink flowers. Blooms in the summer and is useful for container growing. To 1.2 m × 90 cm (4 × 3 ft). A very old rose, cultivated in gardens since at least 1800.

'Rambling Rector'
Rambler, with many dense clusters of small, single, white flowers crowned with bright gold stamens. Sweetly scented, the foliage is downy grey-green. Flowers in the summer only, but it is vigorous and prolific; a good rose to train into trees or along hedges. Will grow against a north wall or in dappled shade. To 6 m (20 ft). Less rampageous than 'Kiftsgate'. Very old, but date unknown.

'Rambling Rector'

'Raubritter'

'Reine Victoria'

'Reine Victoria'

Bourbon, the flowers are lilac-pink and neatly globe-shaped, and look as though they are part of an antique Victorian bouquet made of tiny sea shells. It is a fussy rose, however, prone to blackspot and demanding good fertile soil to perform properly. But the fragrance of the flower clusters is so delicious it is worth the extra bother. It makes a small neat bush, 1.2 m × 90 cm (4 × 3 ft), so it can be fussed over in containers. 1872.

R. 'Alba Maxima'

A large straggly shrub up to 2 m (7 ft), this is the 'Great Double White' of the old cottage gardens; it has been grown at least since the fifteenth century. The flowers are large, fully double and pure white although sometimes touched with cream and appear in large clusters amidst the elegant grey-green leaves. New stems spring from the base of the plant and arch gracefully when laden with flowers. To 1.8 m (6 ft)

'Raubritter'

Rambler, with clusters of shell-like, raspberry-pink flowers that appear once during summer in mad profusion, but with only faint perfume. Makes a low sprawling shrub, to 90 cm × 1.8 m (3 × 6 ft); planted in groups to sprawl over low walls it is spectacular. 1936.

'Reine de Violettes'

Hybrid Perpetual, with small burgundy-red flowers that fade to soft violet, retaining their glorious scent to the last petal. It makes an upright shrub, to 1.5 m × 90 cm (5 × 3 ft), and flowers continuously from summer well into autumn. 1860.

'Reine de Violettes'

R. banksiae 'Lutea'

If you want to evoke the gardens of Italy in your rose garden, grow this vigorous climber – it will grow to 6 m (20 ft) – over a pergola-covered terrace. It needs a warm sheltered spot to flourish, but is worth the trouble for the abundant clusters of pale yellow, lemon-scented flowers that appear in early summer.

R. × *centifolia*

Known as the Cabbage Rose or Provence Rose, it is one of the most ancient roses in cultivation, having been grown in European gardens since the sixteenth century. The flowers have a heady perfume and are exceedingly double, hence its common name. It flowers once in summer and will grow in poor soils to 1.8 m (6 ft). 'Bullata' is a form of this old rose with similar flowers produced in heavy trusses on a smaller somewhat tidier plant. The foliage appears crinkled, tinted reddish brown on top.

R. × *centifolia* 'Cristata'
(Chapeau de Napoléon, Crested Moss)

Centifolia, the flowers are warm pink and richly scented. It takes its name from the heavy mossy growth that fringes the calyx, giving it the appearance of a tricorn hat similar to the one worn by the Little Emperor. The bush has a lax habit with the prickly branches bent beneath their floral burden. It flowers in summer only. 1826.

R. × *centifolia* 'Muscosa'
(Common Moss, Old Moss)

Centifolia Moss, with blushing pink, wonderfully double flowers that have a strong perfume. The foliage is large and coarse with a pronounced serrated edge on a lax shrub up to 1.5 × 1.2 m (5 × 4 ft). It flowers during summer only and is one of the oldest garden flowers. Pre-1700.

R. × centifolia 'Muscosa'

R. × *centifolia* 'Variegata'
(synonym 'Village Maid')

Centifolia, with white flowers faintly variegated with splashes of pale lilac-pink. Strongly scented, and pretty when it does not rain since the flowers turn to mush in damp weather. A sprawly, prickly bush to 1.5 × 1.2 m (5 × 4 ft), it really needs support to look good. Flowers repeatedly. 1845.

R. × *damascena bifera*
(Quatre Saisons)

An ancient rose, it is also known as the Autumn Damask. Virgil described it (*c.* 30BC) as the 'twice blooming rose of Paestum', and it has long been revered as the most sweetly scented of all the roses; a must for the pot pourri garden. The flowers are pale pink, loosely double and highly perfumed, set against greyish foliage. It grows to a sprawly shrub up to 1.2 m (4 ft).

Rosa × *damascena versicolor*
(York and Lancaster)

Damask with unusual flowers: on one branch the flowers may be pink, white or splashed and variegated with these colours. The sepals are long and elegant and the flowers sweetly scented. It is repeat-flowering and grows best if given good rich soil, when it will make a bush up to 2 × 2 m (7 × 7 ft). An ancient rose, from before 1551, it is often confused with the Gallica, Rosa Mundi.

R. filipes 'Kiftsgate'

tiny lilac-tinted flowers. Its sprawling habit inclines it to mound-forming ground-cover, up to 1.5 m (5 ft), and it actually likes growing in the dappled shade of woodland gardens.

R. filipes 'Kiftsgate'
Rambler, with trusses of starry, single white flowers that are very strongly scented. It is renowned for its rampant habit, and once established will climb to 9 × 6 m (30 × 20 ft), smothering everything in its path in a floral foam during summer. It takes its name from the famous garden, Kiftsgate Court. 1952.

R. foetida 'Persiana'
A double form of the species; both were used to introduce yellow tints to modern roses. The very double flowers have a faint, some think unpleasant, scent and like many yellow roses it can suffer from black spot. Makes a tall shrub up to 1.8 m (6 ft), thriving in poor soils and full sun.

R. gallica officinalis (**Apothecary's Rose**)
As its common name implies, this was the rose grown for 'physic', and how soothing to be treated with a syrup made from its petals. A small upright growing shrub to 90 cm (3 ft), the dense foliage has a grey-green cast setting off the large crimson flowers to good effect. It flowers once, prolifically, in summer. Like other Gallicas, it can be used to make a hedge.

R. ecae
A dense arched shrub with branches crooked and bent every which way. Its bright egg-yolk yellow single flowers appear from early spring. It requires a warm sunny and sheltered spot with plenty of room to spread, since it will grow to 2.5 m (8 ft).

R. eglanteria (*R. rubiginosa*)
The sweetbriar or Eglantine rose has wonderful apple-scented foliage that is especially noticeable on warm humid summer evenings. For this it makes a delightful addition to hedge plantings. An arching bush up to 3 m (10 ft) with single pink flowers and bright red hips, It will grow on chalk.

R. elegantula 'Persetosa' (**synonym** *R. farreri persetosa*)
Sometimes known as the Threepenny Bit Rose in reference to the smallness of the foliage that flames purple and crimson in autumn. The scarlet hips are small but abundant, following the

R. gallica 'Versicolor'

This is the oldest striped rose, commonly called Rosa Mundi, and known since the sixteenth century. The flowers are striped and blotched with crimson and white and appear profusely in summer. It is often used for low hedges to 90 cm (3 ft), but left unpruned it requires support for the flower-laden branches.

R. glauca (R. rubrifolia)

Its name refers to the purplish-grey tinge of the foliage against which the

R. glauca

tiny single flowers glow like pink stars. The hips also carry the odd colouring. It makes a tall arching shrub to 4 m (12 ft) with few thorns. It has been grown in gardens since 1830, and today its colouring has made it popular in the mixed border.

R. × harisonii 'Harison's Yellow'

With double yellow flowers set amidst small deeply serrated foliage, this is the Yellow Rose of Texas. It has a light sweet scent and blooms once, very early, the flowers dotted the length of the long arching canes. It has a spreading habit to 2 m (7 ft). 1830.

R. × jacksonii 'Max Graf'

Rugosa, flowers once when it is covered with broad dishes of single raspberry-pink flowers with a bold splash of gold stamens in their centres. It is an excellent plant for ground-

R. gallica officinalis

cover; long shoots, up to 2.5 m (8 ft) long, snake along the ground forming a dense mat that once a summer is covered with blossoms. Smells sweetly of apples. 1919.

R. nitida

A native of North America, it is one of the few roses to like damp, acid soil. It suckers freely making dense thickets up to 90 cm (3 ft). The flowers are small single and deep pink, but the dainty fern-like foliage blazes away in autumn.

R. × odorata 'Pallida' (Old Blush China, Parsons' Pink)

China, with shimmering silvery-pink flowers flushed bright pink. Double and highly scented, it is a small bush to about 1.2 m (4 ft), or if trained to climb will reach 2.5 m (8 ft). Flowers continuously and tolerates shade. One of the first China roses introduced to Europe in 1789, and one of the most garden worthy of that group.

R. palustris

A hardy suckering shrub to grow in boggy places, hence its common name of Swamp Rose. The flowers are single and bright pink with bold gold stamens; the buds are girdled by long tapering calyces in a most graceful manner. It makes a tall thicket up to 2.5 m (8 ft) high, flowering throughout the season.

R. pendulina

R. pendulina

After the single, deep pink flowers drop, this low-spreading shrub, to 1.2 m (4 ft), is covered with fat, bottle-shaped, bright red hips dangling from the purplish-red stems. It has a graceful, arching habit and is suited to foreground plantings in woodland gardens.

R. pimpinellifolia

A small bush to 90 cm (3 ft), it will do well in shade and on sandy soils. The flowers are small and white with pronounced stamens, and are followed by shiny black hips. The ferny foliage is rather coarse and the stems are well covered in fine prickly thorns. A good boundary hedge rose.

R. primula

Next to the sweetbriar, this rose has the most wonderfully scented foliage; it is called the Incense Rose which describes its perfume exactly. An upright-growing shrub to 1.5 m (5 ft) it is best if trained against a wall, either below a window or near the door so that on humid summer evenings or after rain the fragrance will fill the room. The small yellow flowers are strongly scented and appear very early. When they drop they leave behind small spidery stamens and calyces amidst the ferny deep green leaves. The branches are mahogany-red and covered in fine thorns.

R. × richardii (R. sancta)

Known commonly as the Holy Rose it is very ancient. The flower garlands found crowning Egyptian mummies of AD200–500 were made from this or a very similar rose. It was introduced to Europe from Abyssinia where it was grown in churchyards and monastery gardens. It makes a neat rounded bush, up to 1.2 m (4 ft), covered in loose clusters of single, palest pink flowers. It will grow in poor soils or damp conditions and is suited to container gardening.

R. 'Scabrosa'

The broad single flowers are cherry red, highly fragrant, and repeat throughout the season. The foliage colours well in autumn and its hips are much the largest of any rose. It will grow in poor soils, including seaside plantings, and its dense upright habit, to 2 m (7 ft), makes it suitable for hedging.

R. 'Sealing Wax'

This and its sister 'Geranium' are selected seedlings of *R. moyesii*, valued in gardens for their vibrantly coloured hips. 'Sealing Wax' has bright pink flowers and 'Geranium' cherry red flowers. Both will grow in poor soils or shade, but a spot where the sun will catch their vivid colouring is preferable. They grow to about 2.5 m (8 ft).

R. sericea pteracantha

This is a good rose for woodland planting, requiring plenty of room to accommodate its eventual 3 m (10 ft) arching branches. But its main feature is the size and colour of the huge thorns, which are broad, flat and translucent red. Plant it where it will catch the sun for the best effect, although it will grow in shade. The single white flowers appear in spring, and the hips and foliage are also attractive. 1890.

R. setigera

Native to North America, from Ontario in the north to Texas and Florida in the south, it is commonly called the Prairie Rose. Its single bright pink flowers appear throughout the summer on long trailing branches up to 5 m (16 ft) long. Use it as ground cover or to blanket low retaining walls; it will grow in poor soils or on the edge of ponds. In the autumn it will be covered in a profusion of small, bright red hips. 'Baltimore Belle'

R. 'Viridiflora'

raised in the USA in 1843 is a hybrid with *R. gallica* and is characterized by a profusion of wonderfully double, pale pink flowers that carry on late into the season.

R. 'Viridiflora'

This is the rose for flower arrangers since the flowers are formed from the numerous green bracts that turn reddish brown as they age. More of a curiosity than a beauty, it is easy to grow, disease free, will tolerate shade and poor soils, and can be grown in containers since it has the small stature of the China roses, to 90 cm (3 ft).

R. willmottiae

Another shrub with a grey bloom to the arching stems and fern-like foliage, which releases a slight fragrance when crushed. The flowers are single and rich lilac-pink, followed by small red hips. It will grow to about 1.8 m (6 ft) and in shade or poor soils.

'Rose de Meaux'

Centifolia, with small, double, pink flowers on a tidy little bush, to 90 × 60 cm (3 × 2 ft). Needs a good soil to do its best, and rewards your attentions with its delicious perfume. An ideal container rose, it flowers only once. 1789.

'Rose de Rescht'

Damask, with bunches of small, very double flowers introduced by Nancy Lindsay, who described it as a 'sturdy, yard high bush of glazed lizard green, perpetually emblazoned with full camellia flowers of pigeon's blood ruby, irised with royal-purple, haloed with dragon sepals...' Her images are hard to better, but the passage does not mention the heady scent. Makes a dense and healthy bush, to 1.2 m × 90 cm (4 × 3ft). Date unknown.

'St Nicholas'

Damask-style, with semi-double flowers that open to saucers of soft raspberry-tinted pink with a bold boss of gold stamens. Prettily scented, it flowers repeatedly and in autumn has clusters of small red hips that blacken with frost and age. An upright shrub, to 1.8 × 1.5 m (6 × 5 ft). Put it at the back of a border with some support. Named for the Yorkshire garden of the Hon. Bobbie and Lady Serena James. 1950.

'Sir Walter Raleigh'

English Rose, with large double flowers, coloured clear warm pink with a strong perfume. Makes an upright leafy bush to 1.2 × 1 m (4 × 3.5 ft). It was named to commemorate the founding of the first English Colony in the New World. 1985.

'Sissinghurst Castle'

Gallica, with velvety, deep-maroon petals that pale to mauve on their outer edges. The flowers are small and sweetly scented and the bush is very twiggy up to 90 × 90 cm (3 × 3 ft). Will grow in the shade and flowers just once. Discovered by Vita Sackville-West at Sissinghurst among the remains of the old garden. Reintroduced 1947.

'Sombreuil' (Colonial White)

Climbing Tea, with brilliant white flowers; the petals are tinted cream at their base. Fully double, repeat-flowering and very fragrant, the blooms are set off by the lush green foliage on a bush that will grow to 2.5 m (8 ft) with support, or trained as a climber. Benefits from a warm sheltered site. 1850.

'Souvenir de la Malmaison'
Bourbon, with peach-tinted, ivory-white flowers, fully double and highly fragrant. It flowers continuously, but is temperamental in wet weather; the damp discourages the flowers and they will not open as prettily as they should. Can make a tall bush to 1.8 × 1.8 m (6 × 6 ft) and should be given the support of a tripod to keep it in bounds. 1843.

'Stanwell Perpetual'
Pimpinellifolia × Damask hybrid, with soft pink, loosely double flowers that have a strong sweet scent. Lives up to its name with a lavish flush of flowers in midsummer. A tall arching shrub with dense, glaucous foliage, it will grow in shade and looks well as foreground planting in a woodland garden. To 1.5 × 1.5 m (5 × 5 ft). 1838.

'Swan'
English Rose, with large, fully double, white flowers that are strongly scented on a sturdy upright bush, to 1.2 m × 90 cm (4 × 3 ft). 1987.

'Swany'
Procumbent, with clusters of very full, ivory-white flowers. It blooms continuously and is ideal ground-cover, or should I say, ground-smothering. To 60 cm × 2.8 m (2 × 9 ft). 1978.

'Trier'
Rambler, with semi-double, creamy-white flowers in dense clusters. This is

'Variegata di Bologna'

more of a tall shrub, but is ideal for training around pillars and pergola supports. Heavily scented and repeat-flowering, it grows to 2.5 × 1.8 m (8 × 6 ft). 1904.

'Tuscany Superb'
Gallica, with large, frilly, double flowers of velvet violet-maroon set off by a heart of golden stamens. Very strongly scented, it flowers only in summer, but is spectacular. Upright growing to 1.2 m × 90 cm (4 × 3 ft), its lush, bright green foliage is a welcome addition to the garden. 1848.

'Variegata di Bologna'
Bourbon, with raspberry splashed and striped cream petals with the characteristic fruity perfume. An upright bush, rather spindly because the foliage is sparse, to 1.5 × 1.2 m (5 × 4 ft), it flowers repeatedly. 1909.

'Wenlock'
English Rose, with shallow, double, cupped flowers in deep wine-red.

Strongly fragrant and flowers prolifically over a long season. A strong growing bush to 1.2 m × 90 cm (4 × 3 ft). 1984.

'The Wife of Bath'
English Rose, with small, cupped, rose-pink flowers strongly scented of myrrh. Flowers repeatedly on a sturdy, dependably hardy bush to 90 × 60 cm (3 × 2 ft). 1969.

'William Lobb' (Old Velvet Moss)
Moss, with clusters of small, deep magenta-red flowers and heavily mossed stems and calyces. Vigorous to 2 × 1.8 m (7 × 6 ft), it looks better with some support. Richly perfumed, it flowers in summer. 1855.

'Wise Portia'
English Rose, with purple to mauve flowers that are highly scented. It makes a small bush, 75 × 75 cm (2.5 × 2.5 ft), and requires good soil and an extra measure of care to do its best. 1982.

'Zéphirine Drouhin'
Bourbon, with bright pink, double flowers that are strongly scented and excellent for making pot pourri. Also known as the Thornless Rose, it is a climber up to 3 m (10 ft), although it can also be grown as a shrub with support. The young growth is a martyr to mildew, so take care early in the season, but it does seem to grow out of this tendency. Repeat-flowering. 1868.

Underplanting and Companion Planting

Acaena caesiiglauca

Ground-covering, spreading sub-shrub with tiny steely-blue leaves on stems that have a purplish tinge. Flowers like little burrs appear on stiff stems in summer. Unusual and effective.

Achillea 'Moonshine'

Silver-leaved perennial with flower heads that are a curious dusty-yellow colour. I do not object to this colour used with wine-tinted roses, or white or ivory and cream, but pink is risky. Some people cut away the flowers the minute they appear, to have only the feathery tussocks of grey foliage. To 60 × 45 cm (2 ft × 18 in).

Anaphalis triplinervis

Grey-leaved perennial with white everlasting flowers; hence the name Pearly Immortelle. During spring and early summer it is a clump of silver, but by midsummer is covered in flower stalks. These can be gathered and dried. To 45 × 30 cm (18 × 12 in).

Artemisia ludoviciana
(synonym A. purshiana)

Invasive spreading perennial; 'Powis Castle', low, mound-forming shrub. These silver-leaved plants are among the best in the garden, although the two spreaders should be used with disgression since they will swamp any

treasure planted with them, but tall roses can withstand the competition. There are any number of these silver-leaved perennials and shrubs that are ideal among the old roses.

Berberis thunbergii atropurpurea

Deciduous shrub with small russet leaves that turn flame-red in autumn. Makes a tall shrub, 1.8 × 1.5 m (6 × 5 ft). The dwarf version, 'Atropurpurea Nana', has the same colouring but is only 60 × 60 cm (2 × 2 ft).

Campanula pyramidalis alba

Perennial with dark-green foliage and spires of pure white flowers during summer. To 90 × 30 cm (3 × 1 ft).

Lilium candidum

Berberis thunbergii atropurpurea

Convallaria majalis

The familiar lily-of-the-valley, it will enjoy the shade of a group of tall-growing shrub roses. In early summer its sweet-scented white flowers complement a canopy of pink or ivory roses, and the rich green foliage makes a good ground-cover.

Cotinus coggygria rubrifolius
'Notcutt's Variety'

The rich violet foliage of this deciduous shrub, 1.8 × 1.5 m (6 × 5 ft), suits purple-tinted roses. The species, *C. coggygria*, has pink-tinted leaves that combine well with strong pink-flowered roses.

Helichrysum petiolare
Grey-leaved spreading shrub, 45 × 60 cm (18 in × 2 ft). There are a few cultivars with yellow, lime-green or variegated foliage.

Juniperus virginiana 'Silver Spreader'
This is just one example among the many evergreen conifers of a low, mound-forming or spreading shrub with a rich glaucous colour. As found-ation planting to a collection of lax roses, or with canes pegged down across their fronds, some pretty effects can be achieved.

Lamium maculatum 'White Nancy'
is the most ghostly of the lamiums, a spreading ground-covering perennial. *L. galeobdolon* 'Silberteppich' is lar-ger and less refined, but just as silvery.

Lavandula 'Munstead'
Dwarf lavender, to 60 × 60 cm (2 × 2 ft); is good for edging and has dark lavender-blue flowers. 'Hidcote' is smaller, to 30 × 45 cm (12 × 18 in), and has the deepest purple flowers and good silver foliage.

Lilium martagon album, L. candidum
To create a cottage garden one must include these oldest of the old lilies. The martagon has small pendant flowers, the petals turning back to resemble an Oriental's turban. Can-didum is the ancient Madonna lily with trumpet-shaped, pure white flowers. Lilies are bulbs requiring well-drained soil and in the case of the Madonna, a sun-baked spot. The mar-tagon will grow in sun or shade and can naturalize itself in the verge of a woodland garden.

Lychnis coronaria alba
Grey, felty rosettes of leaves cover the ground, spreading up to 30 cm (12 in) across. Flower stalks, up to 60 cm (24 ft) tall, appear in summer, studded with starry white blossoms.

Nepeta 'Six Hills Giant'
Grey-leaved shrub with tall, purple flower spikes; it makes a mound 1.2 m × 60 cm (4 × 2 ft). Cut it hard back in spring. *N. mussinii* is the familiar catmint; a smaller version with bluer flowers.

Ribes sanguineum 'Brocklebankii'
Deciduous shrub with the acid-green leaves which are such a good contrast to dark-flowered roses. Makes a tall shrub to 1.8 × 1.5 m (6 × 5 ft).

Rosmarinus × lavandulacea (synonym R. officinalis prostratus)
The familiar herb, rosemary, but in a procumbent form, that makes a neat, ground-covering mat of shiny green leaves. Other sorts of rosemary look well with old roses, especially the white-flowered variety that makes a tidy upright shrub to 1.2 m (4 ft).

Nepeta 'Six Hills Giant'

Salvia officinalis 'Purpurascens'

Ruta graveolens 'Jackman's Blue'

Shrubby herb to 60 × 30 cm (2 × 1 ft) with rounded glaucous foliage that has a pungent scent when crushed. Clip away the greenish yellow flowers as they appear and cut hard back in spring to keep tidy.

Salvia officinalis 'Purpurascens'

Purple sage, another shrubby herb with grey foliage that has a deep purple tint when young. Produces spires of bright purple bracts. Clip over every spring to keep tidy. It has a low spreading habit, 60 × 90 cm (2 × 3 ft).

Saxifraga × *urbium* 'Aureopunctata'

Mat-forming, spreading, evergreen ground-cover of small leathery rosettes; dark green, splashed with lemon yellow. In summer the tiny pink flowers appear, held on erect stems; they float over the mottled carpet like foam on an ice-cream soda.

Species geraniums

These are the hardy geraniums that come in many sizes and colours, from pure white through pink to clear blue and bright violet. All of them are suitable for growing among old roses, and form ground-covering mats, sending up their flowers among the branches and flower clusters.

Stachys byzantina 'Silver Carpet'

A non-flowering species of the grey, woolly-leaved perennial commonly called lamb's ears. There are over half-a-dozen named varieties, including a good citrus-green, 'Primrose Heron', that would look well with deep-red and maroon roses.

Geranium macrorrhizum 'Ingwersen's Variety'

Stachys byzantina 'Silver Carpet'

Thymus × *citriodorus* 'Argenteus'

Silver variegated thyme, a petite shrubby herb with creamy-white variegated leaves. Plant in clumps of three or five for best effect. Makes a low ground-covering mat, 20 × 30 cm (8 × 12 in).

Viburnum plicatum 'Lanarth'

Low-growing deciduous shrub that has creamy-white flower heads like saucers held at the tips of outstretched tiers of branches. A very graceful shrub, to 1.8 × 2.5 m (6 × 8 ft). A good support to let lax-growing roses re-cline across.

Viola cornuta alba

Mat-forming perennial; violet with large, pure white flowers like a butterfly's wings.

BIBLIOGRAPHY

Beales, Peter, *Classic Roses*, Collins Harvill, London 1985; Rinehart and Wilson, New York 1985

Bunyard, E.A., *Old Garden Roses*, Country Life, London 1936

Jekyll, Gertrude, *Roses for English Gardens*, Country Life, London 1902

Phillips, Roger and Rix, Martin, *Roses*, The Pan Garden Plants Series, Pan Books, London 1988

Thomas, Graham Stuart, *The Old Shrub Roses* (rev'd edn), J. M. Dent, London 1980

Underwood, Mrs Desmond, *Grey and Silver Plants*, Collins, London 1971

Verey, Rosemary, *The Scented Garden*, Michael Joseph, London 1981

—— *The Garden in Winter*, Windward, London 1988

Williams, Dorothy Hunt, *Historic Virginia Gardens*, University of Virginia Press, 1975

All About Roses, Ortho Books, New York 1990

Roses, Brooklyn Botanic Garden Record, Plants & Gardens, New York, Spring 1980

Taylor's Guide to Roses, Houghton Miflin Co., New York 1990

LIST OF SUPPLIERS

UK

David Austin Roses
Bowling Green Lane
Albrighton
Wolverhampton WV7 3HB

Peter Beales Roses
London Road
Attleborough
Norfolk NR17 1AY

Le Grice Roses
Norwich Road
North Walsham
Norfolk NR28 0DR

Hilliers Nurseries
(Winchester) Ltd
Ampfield House
Romsey
Herts SO5 9PA

John Mattock Ltd
The Rose Nurseries
Nuneham Courtenay
Oxford OX9 9PY

Warley Rose Gardens
Warley Street
Great Warley
Brentwood
Essex CM13 3JH

The Royal National Rose Society offers an 'Old Rose Group', a quarterly journal, and shows gardens which are open to the general public. Each July it sponsors a rose festival. Membership details from:

Membership Secretary RNRS
Bone Hill
Chiswell Green
St Albans
Herts

USA

The Antique Rose Emporium
Rt 5, Box 143
Brenham
TX 77833

Heritage Rose Gardens
16831 Mitchell Creek Road
Fort Bragg
CA 95437

Pickering Nurseries
670 Kingston Road
Pickering
ON L1V 1A6

Roses of Yesterday and Today
802 Brown's Valley Road
Watsonville
CA 95076-0398

*Wayside Gardens
Hodges
SC 29695

*Jackson & Perkins Ltd
PO Box 808
Tuttin
CA 92681
(*Stockists of David Austin English Roses)

The 'Heritage Roses Group' exists for enthusiasts of old-fashioned roses. Members of the group receive a quarterly newsletter. Apply to:

Lily Shohan
RD1, Box 299
Clinton Corners
NY 12514

INDEX

Numbers in *italics* refer to illustration captions

ACKNOWLEDGEMENTS

To my editor, Coralie Hepburn, I give my heartfelt thanks for her tactful 'phone calls
encouraging and urging me ever onward. But to Shirley Cargill I owe the greatest
debt of gratitude; for her suggestions, advice and friendship, but most of all for creating
one of the loveliest old-fashioned rose gardens in England.

The author and publishers would like to thank the following photographers
and organizations for their permission to reproduce the photographs in this book:
Heather Angel 10–11, 52 right, 61, 68–69, 95 above
David Austin Roses 82 left, 91
Michael Boys 113
Ethne Clarke 12, 13, 15
The Garden Picture Library: Clive Boursnell 34; John Glover 44 below, 89; Marijke Heuff
endpaper; Lamontagne 48 above, 73, 81 inset, 82 right, 87, 100, 102, 104; Marianne
Majerus 21, 40; Joanne Pavia 79; Gary Rogers 28, 30–31; Brigitte Thomas 20, 77.
Jerry Harpur 36–37 (Park Farm, Gt Waltham), 63 inset (designer, Mirabel Osler), 94, 98 above right;
Jacqui Hurst 29, 62–63, 75, 85 left, 88, 92 left, 98 left
Andrew Lawson 1, 2, 3–4, 8, 11 inset, 16, 17, 18–19, 19 inset, 24, 25, 26, 27, 33, 37 inset, 44 above,
48 below, 49, 56 left and right, 57, 83, 84, 85 right, 86 left, 90, 92 right, 93, 95 below,
96–97, 98 right, 101 left and right, 103, 105 left and right, 106, 107 left, centre and right,
Di Lewis/EWA 70–71
Marianne Majerus 41, 52 left, 60
Spike Powell/EWA 72
Hazel Le Rougetel/Biofotos 9 left and right, 35, 71 inset, 80–81, 86 right, 99 right
George Wright 6–7, 7 inset, 22–23, 45